《中国节庆文化》丛书
编委会名单

顾 问

史蒂文·施迈德　　冯骥才　　周明甫

黄忠彩　　武翠英　　王国泰

主 编

李 松

副主编

张 刚　彭新良

编 委（按姓氏笔画排列）

王学文　　田阡　　邢莉　　齐勇锋

李旭　　李松　　杨正文　　杨海周

张刚　　张勃　　张跃　　张暖

金蕾　　赵学玉　　萧放　　彭新良

List of Members of Editorial Board
of *Chinese Festival Culture Series*

中国节庆文化丛书

Chinese Festival Culture Series

The Peony Festival

主　编　李　松
副主编　张　刚　彭新良

牡丹节

彭新良
谭瑾◎著
梁瑞◎译

全国百佳图书出版单位

时代出版传媒股份有限公司

安徽人民出版社

图书在版编目(ＣＩＰ)数据

牡丹节:汉英对照/彭新良,谭瑾著;梁瑞译.—合肥:安徽人民出版社,2014.1
(中国节庆文化丛书/李松,张刚,彭新良主编)

ISBN 978－7－212－07068－7

Ⅰ.①牡⋯　Ⅱ.①彭⋯　②谭⋯　③梁⋯　Ⅲ.①节日—风俗习惯—中国—
汉、英　Ⅳ.①K892.1

中国版本图书馆 CIP 数据核字(2013)第 315319 号

Zhongguo Jieqing Wenhua Congshu　Mudanjie

中国节庆文化丛书　**牡丹节**

李　松　**主编**　张　刚　彭新良　**副主编**

彭新良　谭　瑾　**著**　梁　瑞　**译**

出 版 人:朱寒冬　　　　　　图书策划:胡正义　丁怀超　李　旭
责任编辑:陈　娟　　　　　　装帧设计:宋文岚

出版发行:时代出版传媒股份有限公司 http://www.press-mart.com
　　　　安徽人民出版社 http://www.ahpeople.com
　　　　合肥市政务文化新区翡翠路 1118 号出版传媒广场八楼
　　　　邮编:230071
　　　　营销部电话:0551-63533258　0551-63533292(传真)
制　　版:合肥市中旭制版有限责任公司
印　　制:安徽新华印刷股份有限公司

开本:710×1010　1/16　　　印张:11.25　　　　字数:200 千
版次:2014 年 3 月第 1 版　　2016 年 7 月第 3 次印刷

标准书号:ISBN 978－7－212－07068－7　　　定价:20.00 元

Our Common Days

(Preface)

The most important day for a person in a year is his or her birthday, and the most important days for all of us are the festivals. We can say that the festivals are our common days.

Festivals are commemorating days with various meanings. There are national, ethnic and religious festivals, such as the National Day and Christmas Day, and some festivals for certain groups, such as the Women's Day, the Children's Day and the Labor Day. There are some other festivals closely related to our lives. These festivals have long histories and different customs that have been passed on from one generation to another. There are also different traditional festivals. China is a country full of 56 ethnic groups, and all of the ethnic groups are collectively called the Chinese Nation. Some traditional festivals are common to all people of the Chinese Nation, and some others are unique to certain ethnic groups. For example, the Spring Festival, the Mid-Autumn Day, the Lantern Festival, the Dragon Boat Festival, the Tomb-Sweeping Day and the Double-Ninth Day are common festivals to all of the Chinese people. On the other hand, the New Year of the Qiang Ethnic (a World Cultural Heritage), for example, is a unique festival to the

我们共同的日子

（代序）

个人一年一度最重要的日子是生日，大家一年一度最重要的日子是节日。节日是大家共同的日子。

节日是一种纪念日，内涵多种多样。有民族的、国家的、宗教的，比如国庆节、圣诞节等。有某一类人的，如妇女、儿童、劳动者的，这便是妇女节、儿童节、劳动节等。也有与人们的生活生产密切相关的，这类节日历史悠久，很早就形成了一整套人们约定俗成、代代相传的节日习俗，这是一种传统的节日。传统节日也多种多样。中国是个多民族国家，有五十六个民族，统称中华民族。传统节日有全民族共有的，也有某个民族特有的。比如春节、中秋节、元宵节、端午节、清明节、重阳节等，就为中华民族所共用和共享；世界文化遗产羌年就为羌族独有和独享。各民族这样的节日很多。

传统节日是在漫长的农耕时代形成的。农耕时代生产与生活、人与自然的关系十分密切。人们或为了感恩于大自然的恩赐，或为了庆祝辛苦劳作换来的收获，或为了激发生命的活力，或为了加强人际的亲情，经过长期相互认同，最终约定俗成，渐渐把一年中某一天确定为节日，并创造了十分完整又严格的节俗，如仪式、庆典、规制、禁忌，乃至特定的游艺、装饰与食品，来把节日这天演化成一个独具内涵和迷人的日子。更重要的是，人们在每一个传统的节日里，还把共同的生活理想、人间愿望与审美追求融入节日的内涵与种种仪式中。因此，它是中华民族世间理想与生活愿望极致的表现。可以说，我们的传统——精神文化传统，往往就是依靠这代代相传的一年一度的节日继承下来的。

Qiang Ethnic Group, and there are many festivals celebrated only by minorities in China.

The traditional festivals are formed throughout the long agrarian age, during which the relationships between life and production and between the people and the nature were very close. To express the gratitude to the nature for its gifts, or celebrate the harvests from hard works, or stimulate the vitality of life, or strengthen the relationships among people, people would determine one day in a year as a festival with complete and strict customs, such as ceremonies, rules and taboos, special activities, decorations and foods to make the festival a day with unique meanings and charms. More importantly, people would integrate their good wishes into the meanings and ceremonies of the festivals. Therefore, the festivals could represent the ideals and wishes of the people in the best way. It is safe to say that our traditions, more specifically, our spiritual and cultural traditions, are inherited through the festivals year by year.

However, since the 20th century, with the transition from the agricultural civilization to the industrial civilization, the cultural traditions formed during the agrarian age have begun to collapse. Especially in China, during the process of opening up in the past 100 years, the festival culture, especially the festival culture in cities, has been impacted by the modern civilization and foreign cultures. At present, the Chinese people have felt that the traditional festivals are leaving away day by day so that some worries are produced about this. With the diminishing of the traditional festivals, the traditional spirits carried by them will also disappear. However, we are not just watching them disappearing, but actively dealing with them, which could fully represent the self-consciousness of the Chinese people in terms of culture.

In those ten years, with the fully launching of the folk culture heritage rescue program of China, and the promotion of the application for national non-material cultural heritage list, more attention has been paid to the traditional festivals, some of which have been added to the central cultural heritage list. After that, in 2006, China has determined that the second Saturday of June of each year shall be the Cultural Heritage Day, and in 2007, the State Council added three important festivals, namely the Tomb-sweeping Day, the Dragon Boat Festival and the Mid-Autumn Day, as the legal holidays. These decisions have showed that our government

然而，自从二十世纪整个人类进入了由农耕文明向工业文明的过渡，农耕时代形成的文化传统开始瓦解。尤其是中国，在近百年由封闭走向开放的过程中，节日文化——特别是城市的节日文化受到现代文明与外来文化的冲击。当下人们已经鲜明地感受到传统节日渐行渐远，并为此产生忧虑。传统节日的淡化必然使其中蕴含的传统精神随之涣散。然而，人们并没有坐等传统的消失，主动和积极地与之应对。这充分显示了当代中国人在文化上的自觉。

近十年，随着中国民间文化遗产抢救工程的全面展开，国家非物质文化遗产名录申报工作的有力推动，传统节日受到关注，一些重要的传统节日列入了国家文化遗产名录。继而，2006年国家将每年六月的第二个周六确定为"文化遗产日"；2007年国务院决定将三个中华民族的重要节日——清明节、端午节和中秋节列为法定放假日。这一重大决定，表现了国家对公众的传统文化生活及其传承的重视与尊重，同时也是保护节日文化遗产十分必要的措施。

节日不放假必然直接消解了节日文化，放假则是恢复节日传统的首要条件。但放假不等于远去的节日立即就会回到身边。节日与假日的不同是因为节日有特定的文化内容与文化形式。那么，重温与恢复已经变得陌生的传统节日习俗则是必不可少的了。

千百年来，我们的祖先从生活的愿望出发，为每一个节日都创造出许许多多美丽又动人的习俗。这种愿望是理想主义的，所以节日习俗是理想的；愿望是情感化的，所以节日习俗也是情感化的；愿望是美好的，所以节日习俗是美的。人们用合家团聚的年夜饭迎接新年；把天上的明月化为手中甜甜的月饼，来象征人间的团圆；在严寒刚刚消退、万物复苏的早春，赶到野外去打扫墓地，告慰亡灵，

emphasizes and respects the traditional cultural activities and their heritages. Meanwhile, these are important measures to protect festival cultural heritages.

Festivals without holidays will directly harm the festival culture. Holiday is the most important condition for the recovery of a festival, but holiday does not mean that the festival will come back immediately. Festivals are different from holidays because festivals have unique cultural contents and forms. Therefore, it will be necessary to review and recover the customs of the traditional festivals that have become strange to us.

For thousands of years, our ancestors created beautiful and moving customs for each festival based on their best wishes. The customs are ideal, since the wishes are ideal. The customs are emotional, since the wishes are emotional. The customs are beautiful, since the wishes are beautiful. We have the family reunion dinner to receive a new year. We make moon cakes according to the shape of the moon in the mid-autumn to symbolize the reunion of our family. We visit the tombs of our ancestors in the early spring and go outing to beautiful and green hills to express our grief. These beautiful festival customs have offered us great comfort and peace for generations.

To ethnic minorities, their unique festivals are of more importance, since these festivals bear their common memories and represent their spirits, characters and identities.

Who ever can say that the traditional customs are out of date? If we have forgotten these customs, we should review them. The review is not imitating the customs of our ancients, but experiencing the spirits and emotions of the traditions with our heart.

During the course of history, customs are changing, but the essence of the national tradition will not change. The tradition is to constantly pursue a better life, to be thankful to the nature and to express our best wishes for family reunion and the peace of the world.

This is the theme of our festivals, and the reason and purpose of this series of books.

The planning and compiling of the series is unique. All of the festivals are held once a year. Since China is a traditional agricultural society,

表达心中的缅怀，同时戴花插柳，踏青春游，亲切地拥抱大地山川……这些诗意化的节日习俗，使我们一代代人的心灵获得了美好的安慰与宁静。

对于少数民族来说，他们特有的节日的意义则更加重要。节日还是他们民族集体记忆的载体、共同精神的依托、个性的表现、民族身份之所在。

谁说传统的习俗过时了？如果我们淡忘了这些习俗，就一定要去重温一下传统。重温不是表象地模仿古人的形式，而是用心去体验传统中的精神与情感。

在历史的进程中，习俗是在不断变化的，但民族传统的精神本质不应变。这传统就是对美好生活不懈的追求，对大自然的感恩与敬畏，对家庭团圆与世间和谐永恒的企望。

这便是我们节日的主题，也是这套节庆丛书编写的根由与目的。

这套书的筹划独具匠心。所有节日都是一年一次。由于我国为传统农耕社会，所以生活与生产同步，节日与大自然的节气密切相关。本丛书以一年的春、夏、秋、冬四个时间板块，将纷繁的传统节日清晰有序地排列开来，又总揽成书，既包括全民族共有的节日盛典，也把少数民族重要的节日遗产纳入其中，以周详的文献和生动的传说，将每个节日的源起、流布与习俗，亦图亦文、有滋有味地娓娓道来。一节一册，单用方便，放在一起则是中华民族传统节日的一部全书，既有知识性、资料性、工具性，又有阅读性和趣味性。这样一套丛书不仅是对我国传统节日的一次总结，也是对传统节日文化富于创意的弘扬。

　　我读了书稿，心生欣喜，因序之。

冯骥才

2013.12.25

the life is synchronized with production, and the festivals are closely relevant to the climates. In this series, all of the traditional festivals in China will be introduced in the order of the four seasons, covering the common festivals as well as important ethnic festivals that have been listed as cultural heritages. All of the festivals are described in detail with texts and images to introduce their origins, customs and distribution. Each book of the series is used to introduce one festival so that it is convenient to read individually and it may be regarded as a complete encyclopedia if connected with each other. Therefore, it is not only intellectual, informative and instrumental, but also readable and interesting. The series could be used as a tool book or read for leisure. It is not only the summary of the traditional festivals of our country, but an innovative promotion of our traditional festival culture.

I felt very delighted after reading the manuscript, so I wrote this preface.

Feng Jicai

December 25th, 2013

目　录 / Contents

第一章

国花牡丹

　　我国以中华命名，"华"者，"花"也，可见中华民族是一个爱花的民族，爱美的民族，花之美好，雅俗共赏。而"花魁"牡丹，以其雍容华贵之姿，千百年来备受国人钟爱与称誉，谓之"国色天香"之花。十三朝古都的历史文化名城洛阳是我国的牡丹花城，其适宜的气候、肥沃的土壤，加之古都所独有的人文环境，使得洛阳牡丹花最负盛名。牡丹花开之时，花开如海，人似潮涌，边游边赏，且歌且行，咏词作赋，起舞花间，皆成洛阳牡丹花会之胜景。牡丹因洛阳名甲天下，洛阳因牡丹增辉添彩。牡丹与牡丹花节已经成为洛阳重要的城市形象代表，牡丹文化已经成为洛阳文化的重要组成部分。

Chapter One

National Flower Peony

China is called Zhong Hua in Chinese (Zhong means the middle and Hua means glorious). Before the Wei-jin and Southern and Northern Dynasty, Hua also meant flower. It thus can be inferred that Chinese people have a fondness for flowers and beauty since ancient times. Though all beauties of flowers are appreciated by people from all walks of life, peony, as the king of flowers, receives the most admiration and praise for hundreds of years for its elegance, beauty and fragrance. The capital of peony in China is Luoyang, a historical and cultural city and capital of thirteen dynasties in history. Its suitable climate, fertile soil and unique culture as an ancient city, make Luoyang peony well-known in the world. When Luoyang peony flowers are in full blossom, they form a flower sea, with visitors walking, appreciating, singing, dancing and poetizing in it. The flowers and people there compose a wonderful scene during the peony festival. Thanks to Luoyang, peony becomes famous in China and thanks to peony, Luoyang becomes more charming. Peony and peony festival have become the symbol of Luoyang and peony culture forms an important part of Luoyang culture.

1 牡丹花的历史传奇
The Legendary History of Peony

As a precious woody plant native to China, peony ranks first among the top ten traditional flowers in China for its large flower, beautiful shape, bright color and pleasant aroma. Being praised as the king of flowers with national beauty and celestial fragrance, it has been regarded as a symbol of richness, luck and prosperity since ancient times and has its own unique, rich and glamorous culture. For Chinese people, peony is the emblem of beauty, purity and love. Country's prosperity, family's richness and peace, and people's happiness and auspiciousness are also thought to be the incarnation of peony.

牡丹是我国特有的木本名贵花卉，因其花大、形美、色艳、香浓而位居十大传统名花之首，有"花中之王""国色天香"的美称，长期以来被视为富贵吉祥、繁荣兴旺的象征。在中国的传统文化里，牡丹早已超脱其物质外形，形成了底蕴深厚、内涵丰富、魅力非凡的牡丹文化。在人民群众的心目中，牡丹是美的化身，纯洁与爱情的象征。国尊繁荣昌盛，家重富贵平安，人喜幸福吉祥，这些特点和寓意，牡丹兼而有之。

牡丹，原为陕、川、鲁、豫以及西藏、云南等一带山区的野生灌木，散生于海拔1500米左右的山坡和林缘，属芍药科植物。在我国古代，牡丹与芍药并未分开命名，郑樵《通志》中说："牡丹初无名，依芍药得名。"因牡丹是灌木木本，故被称为木芍药，芍药属于蓄根草本，被称为草芍药。《诗经·郑风·溱洧》中有诗句云："维士与女，伊其将谑，赠之以芍药。"后人根据诗中所描绘的季节日期推算，此中所记载之芍药应该是木芍药，即牡丹花。古时恋人依依惜别之际，采摘牡丹相赠寄语相思之情，因此，古时牡丹还被称为"将离"，成为情人之间传递爱恋的爱情之花。

1972年，在甘肃武威市柏树乡考古发现的东汉早期圹墓医简中，记录了牡丹治疗"血瘀病"的处方。这是牡丹正式以"牡丹"之名出现于史书中的最早记载。

Originally known as wild shrubs in Shaanxi, Sichuan, Shandong, Henan, Tibet and Yunan, peony grew sparsely on mountains and slopes at around 1500 meters above sea level, and is in the genus Paeonia. In ancient time, peony and Chinese peony, or paeonia lactiflora were both called Shao Yao (Chinese peony) in Chinese. According to *Tong Zhi (A General History)* by Zheng Qiao, "Peony did not have its own name at first and was called Shao Yao like Chinese peony". As peony is a woody plant, it was called Mu Shao Yao (woody Chinese peony), while Chinese peony is a herbaceous plant and was called Cao Shao Yao (herbaceous Chinese peony). In *Book of Songs*, there is a line saying, "Young boys and girls, happily playing together, presents his/her lover a Chinese peony flower." Based on the time the poem described, critics believed that the Chinese peony flower here must be Mu Shao Yao, i.e. peony. In ancient times, when two lovers had to separate, they would give a peony flower to their beloveds to show lovesickness. Therefore, peony was also called Jiang Li (leaving) in ancient China and was a flower of love that shows lovers' attachment.

The earliest record of Mu Dan (current Chinese name of peony) was found in a medical bamboo book written in the early Eastern Han Dynasty, which was discovered in Baishu County, Wuwei City, Gansu Province in 1972. It records a prescription using peony to cure blood stasis. Another medical book *Shennong's Herbal Classics* also describes the medicinal value of peony, "Peony, also named Lu Jiu and Shu Gu, tastes pungent and is cold in nature. Usually growing in mountains and valleys, it can be used to cure blood stasis and nourish internal organs." *The Inner Cannon of Huang Di* says, "Five days after Tomb-Sweeping Day (around April 5th), the field mice are seen like quails and peony flowers blossom." Peony was also referred as Lu Jiu, Shu Gu, Pin Mu, Bai Liang Jin, Tang Shi Zi, etc. in other medical books. From these we can see that its medicinal value has been noticed since ancient times.

During the Southern and Northern Dynasties, peony began to be planted for ornamental use. *Imperial Readings of the Taiping Era* quoted Xie Lingyun's words saying, "Many tree peonies are planted near waters or among bamboos in Yongjia county." Wei Xuan wrote in *Liu Bing Ke Jia Hua Lu (Quotations from Liu Yuxi)* that, "The peony painted by Yang Zihua of the Northern Qi Dynasty has clear contour." Since it had been painted in pictures, it is certain that peony was an ornamental plant during that time. In the Sui Dynasty, Emperor Yang built palaces in Luoyang and planted many precious flowers in imperial gardens. Han Wu depicted it in *Sui Yang Di Hai Shan Ji (History During Emperor Yang's Reign)*, "Yizhou of Hebei Province presented 20 boxes of tree peonies to the emperor, including Fei Lai Hong (rosy cloud), Yuan Jia Hong (Yuan's red), Zui Yan Hong (drunken beauty), Yun Hong (red cloud), Tian Wai Hong (sky red), Yi Fu Huang

《神农本草经》中也记载了牡丹的药用价值："味辛寒，一名鹿韭，一名鼠姑，生山谷。除症结瘀血，安五脏。"《黄帝内经·素问》则载："清明次五日，田鼠化为鴽牡丹华。"在各类药典中，鹿韭、鼠姑、牝牡、百两金、唐狮子等皆指牡丹。可见牡丹的药用价值也很早就已受到人们的关注。

牡丹作为观赏植物始自南北朝时期，文献多有记载。谢灵运在《太平御览》中称"永嘉水际竹间多牡丹"，韦绚在《刘宾客嘉话录》中云："北齐杨子华有画牡丹极分明"，牡丹既已入画，其作为观赏的对象已确切无疑。而至隋朝，隋炀帝于洛阳兴修宫苑，选名贵花卉入植皇家花园，韩屋《隋炀帝海山记》（唐）中记载："易州（今河北省易县）进二十箱牡丹。有'飞来红''袁家红''醉颜红''云红''天外红''一拂黄''软条黄''延安黄''先春红''颤凤娇'等名。"可见当时的牡丹已被人工栽培，并且品种繁多，成为众所周知的名贵花卉。此时不仅明确地将牡丹与芍药分开，并已有"牡丹花王，芍药花相"之称。《隋志·素问篇》中说道："清明次五时，牡丹华。"隋朝可说是牡丹栽培的发展时期。

而牡丹成为花王与国花的繁荣时期是唐朝。唐朝富裕兴盛，文化开放，社会生活多姿多彩，雍容华贵的牡丹特别受到当时世人的追捧，不论富贵贫贱，皆喜观赏牡丹。唐朝定都长安，其皇家园林中依然广种牡丹。唐代牡丹的栽培技术也有了长足的进步，不仅花色繁多（如《酉阳杂俎》载："兴唐寺有牡丹一窠，元和中着花一千二百朵，其色有正晕、倒晕、浅红、浅紫、紫白、白檀等，独无深红，又有花叶中无抹心者，重台花者，其花面七、八寸。"），

(light yellow), Ruan Tiao Huang (soft yellow), Yan An Huang (Yan'an yellow), Xian Chun Hong (early spring red), Chan Feng Jiao (delicate beauty), etc." This indicates that peony during that period had been cultivated for ornamental purpose, had many species, and was regarded as one of the precious flowers. At that time, peony was clearly separated from Chinese peony and the two were praised as The King of Flowers and The Prime Minister of Flowers respectively. In Chapter Suwen, *Sui Zhi (Classics and Ancient Books of the Sui Dynasty)* has "Peony flowers blossom five days after Tomb-sweeping Day". All these records indicate that peony planting had a rapid development in the Sui Dynasty.

The heyday of peony being titled as the king of flowers and national flower is the Tang Dynasty. During that period, China was very prosperous, with rich social activities and open mind toward different cultures. Peony, because of its elegance and beauty, got much admiration from people of different classes. The capital of the Tang Dynasty was moved to Chang'an (today's Xi'an), and peony was still widely planted in imperial gardens. During the Tang Dynasty, peony cultivation techniques were largely improved. Peony not only had various colors, but also gained new species with multi-layer petals. According to *You Yang Za Zu (Miscellaneous Morsels from Youyang)*, "The tree peony in Xingtang Temple had one thousand and two hundred flowers blooming in years of Yuanhe (806-820). The colors of flowers included pink, light purple, purple, white, but no dark red. Some of the flowers did not have stamen or pistil and some had muti-layer petals, as tall as several centimeters." Among all peony species with muti-layer petals, Zuo Zi (Zuo's purple) was the most famous. *Du Yang Za Zu (Miscellaneous Morsels of Duyang)* also recorded the prosperity of peony, "During the reign of Emperor Mu, thousands of tree peonies were planted before the palace. When flowers bloomed, their fragrance was borne by the wind everywhere. One tree peony there had around one thousand leaves and its flowers were large and red." These records testify that peony the with multi-layer petals had been developed in China since the 8th century. According to *Yang Fei Wai Zhuan (Anecdotes of Concubine Yang)*, Li Bai, one of the most famous poets of the Tang Dynasty once wrote three poems on white, purplish red and light red peony to praise the beauty of Concubine Yang of Emperor Xuan, "Her robe is as light as cloud and her face is as beautiful as flowers. With spring breeze blowing, a few dewdrops rolled on the fragrant petals. " His lines made peony well known in China. During the reign of Emperor Jing, Li Zhengfeng wrote that,

还选育出重瓣品种，且以"左紫"驰名。《杜阳杂俎》中记录道："穆宗皇帝殿前种千叶牡丹，花始开香气袭人，一朵千叶，大而且红。"由此可见，我国早在公元9世纪就已栽培出了重瓣牡丹。据乐史《杨妃外传》记载，唐玄宗时，李白为牡丹填写新词，赋清平乐三首，极写纯白、红紫、浅红等三色牡丹的丰姿秀色，以牡丹之美，赞誉杨贵妃之美貌。"云想衣裳花想容，春风拂槛露华浓。"由此牡丹之名大噪。唐敬宗时，李正封咏牡丹诗云："国色朝酣酒，天香夜染

衣。"牡丹遂有"国色天香"的誉称，更加身价百倍。唐朝繁荣时期，世人对牡丹的喜爱已达到狂热的程度，使得牡丹越来越融入人们社会生活的方方面面，以花入衣、以花入饰、以花入馔、以花入俗、以花入文、以花入情，可以说，牡丹已成为代表唐代文化的符号之一，牡丹"国色"是大唐盛世最美的颜色。

到宋朝时，牡丹栽培中心移至洛阳，洛阳牡丹名冠天下。洛阳人特别推崇牡丹，养花、赏花成为风尚。李格非《洛阳名园记》（宋）中载："洛阳花甚多种，而独名牡丹曰花。"当时育种技术有很大提高，运用嫁接法固定和繁殖苗木，新品种不断涌现，所以欧阳修当年曾惊呼："四十年间花百变！"在此基础上，关于牡丹的专著先后问世。像欧阳修的《洛阳牡丹记》《洛阳牡丹图诗》，周诗厚的《洛阳牡丹记》《洛阳花木记》，张峋的《洛

"Its national beauty like spirits intoxicates me in the morning and its celestial fragrance scents my clothes at night." Being praised as having national beauty and celestial fragrance, peony became more popular than before. People's love for peony in the Tang Dynasty was so deep that peony was involved in every aspect of their life. From clothes to accessories, from food to customs, and from paintings to poems, peony can be seen everywhere. It is not exaggerated to say that peony is a symbol of Tang culture and its national beauty is the most gorgeous representative of the Tang Dynasty.

During the Song Dynasty, the center of peony planting was moved back to Luoyang, and Luoyang peony became known as the best in China. Luoyang people were very fond of peony and it was a fashion for them to plant and appreciate peony. Li Gefei, a writer of the Song Dynasty wrote in *Famous Gardens of Luoyang* that, "Though there are many kinds of flowers in Luoyang, people only regard peony as the flower." The breeding techniques of peony at that time were developed greatly and people began to use grafting to breed new species and plant saplings. Ouyang Xiu, a famous writer in the Song Dynasty once exclaimed, "Peony gained a hundred new species in only forty years!" With such development, many works on peony came out, such as *Luoyang Peony* and *Paintings and Poems of Luoyang Peony* by Ouyang Xiu, *Luoyang Peony* and *Flowers and Woods of Luoyang* by Zhou Shihou, and *Luoyang Flowers* by Zhang Xun. These works listed plenty of peony species, described the cultivation techniques, and summarized a set of experience on peony planting.

In the end of the Northern Song Dynasty, many tree peonies in Luoyang were gradually deserted due to constant chaos caused by wars and Chenzhou (southeast of Henan Province) became the new center of peony planting. Zhang Bangji's *Chenzhou Peony* says, "Luoyang peony species are recorded in books, but they are not as luxuriant and diversified as those in Chenzhou. Farmers there plant peony like crops, with the planting area amounting to several hectares." During the Southern Song Dynasty, the center of peony planting was further moved south to Tianpeng (today's Pengzhou, Sichuan Province), Chengdu, Hangzhou and other cities in the south of China. Tianpeng peony was the best in Sichuan and Tianpeng was therefore called the second west capital. Lu You, a famous poet went to Tianpeng in 1178 when he was an official in Sichuan and wrote *Tianpeng Peony*. After the national capital was moved to Hangzhou, peony in Hangzhou developed and gained some new species, such as Chong Tai Jiu Xin Dan Zi Mu Dan (light purple peony with multi-layer of petals) and Bai Hua Qing Yuan Mu Dan (white heart with green rim).

Peony planting encountered its setbacks in the Yuan Dynasty. There were few good species and multi-layer-petal peony could not be found. Yao Sui, a writer of the Yuan Dynasty once sighed in *Preface for Peony*, "To find a multi-layer-petal peony is as

阳花谱》，均列举了大量的牡丹品种，并记述了牡丹的栽培管理，总结出一整套较为完整的成熟经验。

北宋末年，战乱不断，洛阳牡丹栽培开始衰落，陈州牡丹取而代之，张邦基撰《陈州牡丹记》云："洛阳牡丹之品见于花谱，然未若陈州牡丹之盛且多也。圃户花如种黍粟，动以顷计。"南宋时，牡丹栽培中心由北方洛阳移向南方的天彭（今四川省彭州市）、成都、杭州等地。天彭栽培的牡丹，为蜀中第一，号称"小西京"。1178年，诗人陆游在蜀中做官，亲往游赏，并撰《天彭牡丹谱》。宋室南渡后，杭州牡丹得到发展，出现一些新奇品种，如"重台九新淡紫牡丹""白花青缘牡丹"等。

元代是中国牡丹发展的低潮时期，好品种已屈指可数，品种退化，重瓣品种难得一见，因有"千叶独难遇，亦犹千人为英，万人为杰，尤世纪不恒有者"（姚燧《序牡丹》）之叹！

明代，牡丹的栽培中心移至安徽亳州。夏之臣《评亳州牡丹》云："吾亳州牡丹，年来浸盛，娇容三变，尤在季孟之间。等此而上，有天香一品，石榴红，胜娇容，宫红袍，琉璃贯珠，新红种种不一，杂红最后出，品种难得。又有大黄一种，轻腻可爱，不减三变。佛顶青为白色第一。大抵红花以花子红，银红、桃红为上。"又云："草堂数武之步，种葑殆偏，率以两色并作一丛，红白异状，错综其间，又以平头紫，庆天香，先春红三色插入其花丛，间集而成文章，他时盛开灿然若锦。"此时开中国插花技术之先河。

明代，亳州牡丹虽有盛名，但曹州（今山东菏泽）、国都北京的牡

hard as to find a hero among thousands of people. They have rarely appeared for one hundred years."

During the Ming Dynasty, the center of peony cultivation was moved to Bozhou, Anhui Province. Xia Zhichen's *Comment on Bozhou Peony* says that, "Bozhou peony species have grown better and better year by year. Even Jiao Rong San Bian (three colors) is just of average level. Tian Xiang Yi Pin (top fragrance), Shi Liu Hong (garnet), Sheng Jiao Rong (Lady-beauty), Gong Hong Pao (imperial red robe), Liu Li Guan Zhu (bead in white glaze) and Xin Hong (new red) are all better than it. Za Hong (mixed red) is the most rare one among red peony species and Da Huang (bright yellow) is as lovely as Jiao Rong San Bian. Of all white peony species, Fo Ding Qing (Buddha peony) is regarded as the best and colors of purplish red, light rosy and pink are valued most for red ones." Xia also mentioned flower arrangement, "If you plant red and white peony flowers together near your house, adding several purple, pink and rosy ones among them, it will look both bright and gorgeous when they are all in full blossom. " This marks the beginning of flower arrangement in China.

Besides Bozhou, peony species in Caozhou (today's Heze, Shandong Province) and Beijing, the new capital of Ming Dynasty, also embraced their new boom. Taihu Lake district, Lanzhou and Linxia in the northwest of China became famous for their peony, too. Both Caozhou and Bozhou introduced peony during the reign of Emperor Jiajing (1522-1567) and reached the peak of peony planting during the reign of Emperor Wanli (1573-1620). Moreover, they exchanged their peony species frequently. According to Yu Pengnian's *Caozhou Peony*, most peony species in Caozhou were from Bozhou. Baozhou also introduced a lot from Caozhou. *The History of Peony in Bozhou* recorded one of the best species at that time, Jin Yu Jiao Hui (Gold & Jade) and said that it was introduced from Caozhou. Ren Ji Hong (Renji red) and Ping Shi Hong (Pingshi red) also came from Caozhou. It is said in *Caozhou Peony* that during the Ming Dynasty, peony in the south of Caozhou was the best in China.

Since the Liao Dynasty and Jin Dynasty moved their capital to Beijing, peony planting gradually gained popularity there. *The History of Beijing* written in the Ming Dynasty recorded that Emperor Sheng of Liao once appreciated peony in Eternal Spring Palace in March, 994 (Year of Tonghe). During the Ming Dynasty, peony planting was more popular than before and peony flowers were planted around palaces. There were three famous peony gardens outside Beijing: Liang's Garden, Qinghua Garden and Hui' an Garden.

丹栽培也逐渐繁盛起来，江南太湖周围，西北的兰州、临夏也有所发展。曹州与亳州皆于明代嘉靖年间（公元1522—1567年）引入牡丹，也同于万历年间（公元1573—1620年）达到繁盛。两地之间相互交换品种，（清）余鹏年《曹州牡丹谱》中记载："曹花多移自亳。"亳州也引进不少曹州名品，如《亳州牡丹史》中记载一种"金玉交辉"的品种，说是："曹州所出，为第一品。"又有"忍济红""萍实红"两种，也产于曹州。《曹南牡丹谱》亦云："至明曹南牡丹甲于海内。"

北京自辽、金建都于此，牡丹栽培日渐兴盛。明代的《北京考》上记载辽圣宗在统和十二年（公元994年）三月去长春宫观赏牡丹。在明代，牡丹栽培极盛，金殿内外尽植牡丹。城外还有三大名园梁家园、清华园和惠安园。

在江南，明代以江阴牡丹为盛。此外杭州、苏州、上海也有不少种植。广西灌阳也产牡丹，据明代《广西通志》记载，在广西"牡丹出灵川、灌阳，灌阳牡丹有高一丈者，其地名小洛阳"。

到了清代，皇宫内鲜花四季不断，牡丹成为时令摆设。据传清朝慈禧太后非常喜欢牡丹，曾将牡丹定为国花，她命人在故宫御花园和其他园林中种了许多牡丹，并于颐和园修筑国花台。北京的牡丹一般是从曹州购进，一部分盆栽作促成栽培供春节用，一部分植于圃地，出售苗木。清代的牡丹栽培以曹州最盛。《曹县志》云："牡丹非土产也，初盛于雒下（今陕西省雒南县），再盛于亳州，彼时已六七百种，分五色排列，叙至于今，亳州寂寥，而盛事悉归曹州。""曹州园户种花如种黍粟，动以顷计，盖连畦接畛也。"（《曹州牡丹谱》）蒲松龄在

In the south of the Yangtze River, peony in Jiangyin was regarded as the best. Hangzhou, Suzhou and Shanghai also planted many tree peonies. Guanyang, Guangxi was known for its peony, too. According to *The History of Guangxi* written in the Ming Dynasty, "Peony grows well in Lingchuan and Guanyang. Some tree peonies in Guanyang can be as tall as more than three meters and Guanyang therefore is named as Second Luoyang."

In the Qing Dynasty, flowers of four seasons were planted surrounding the imperial palace and peony became a common ornament plant. It is said that the Empress Dowager Cixi was very fond of peony and even designated it as the national flower. She once asked her servants to plant many tree peonies in imperial gardens of the Forbidden City and she even built a platform of national flower for peony in the Summer Palace. Most peonies in Beijing were bought from Caozhou, some of which were planted in flowerpots for appreciating and others were planted in gardens to sell saplings. The center of peony cultivation at that time was Caozhou. According to *The History of Caozhou*, "Peony did not originally grow in Caozhou. It was first found in Luoxia (Today's Luonan), Shaanxi Province, and became prosperous in Bozhou with five colors and more than six hundred species. But now Bozhou is no longer the center and all fame of peony now belongs to Caozhou." *Caozhou Peony* says that, "Farmers in Caozhou plant peony like planting crops, with hectares' planting areas." Pu Songling's *Strange*

Stories from a Chinese Studio also mentions that Caozhou peony was the best in Shandong Province. At that time, most villages in the northeast of Caozhou planted peony. Farmers there used peony planting to make a living and had their own peony gardens. Villages like Wang Li Zhuang, Hong Miao, Mao Zhuang and Zhao Lou had the best tree peonies. During the reign of the emperor Daoguang (1821-1851), a farmer called Zhao Yutian built his garden in the north of the village to plant peony and Chinese peony, gathering the best species there. As the garden was surrounded by mulberry trees, it was named Sang Li Yuan (mulberry-fenced garden). Zhao in *Peony of Mulberry-Fenced Garden* described 151 peony species and said, "Among ten prefectures and two counties in the east of the mountain, Caozhou owns the best peony. And among ten towns and one city in Caozhou, Heze has the best." "Though there are countless towns and villages in Heze, the best place to plant peony is its north, which is no more than five kilometers long in the south of Lushan Mountain and outside Fan Causeway." Later, another works *Qi Garden Peony* listed more than 140 peony species. At that time, the total planting area of peony reached over 500 *mu* (more than 30 hectares) and more than one hundred thousand tree peonies in Caozhou were transported to Guangzhou, Tianjin, Beijing, Hankou, Xi'an, Jinan and other cities every year. Among these cities, Guangzhou bought the most. There was a proverb in Caozhou: "to plant fruit trees, you'd better plant papaw and persimmon. And to grow flowers, you'd better grow peony and Chinese peony." Thanks

他写的《聊斋志异》一书中，也曾有"曹州牡丹甲齐鲁"的记述。这时，曹州城东北各村栽培牡丹已很普遍。有以养花为业者，成园成圃者很多，其中尤以王李庄、洪庙、毛庄、赵楼各村最兴。道光年间(公元1821—1851年)赵玉田在村北建花园，专养牡丹、芍药，集本村之大成，园之周围树之以桑为篱，名曰"桑篱园"。著有《桑篱园牡丹谱》，其中记述了151种牡丹，内称："山左十郡二州，语牡丹则曹州独也。曹州十邑一州，语牡丹则菏泽独也。""菏泽为郡为里者，不知其几，语牡丹之出，惟有城北之一隅，鲁山之阳，范堤之外，连延褭不能十里。"其后，有《绮园牡丹谱》，核其名者百四十有奇。当时牡丹栽培面积已有500多亩，每年输出十余万株，被运往广州、天津、北京、汉口、西安、济南等地出售。其中运往广州者为最多。当地农民流传着这样一句民谚："种果树莫若木瓜、柿子，养花木还是牡丹、芍药。"再加上社会上的爱好，曹州人善于种花以及牡丹根皮可供药用，所以曹州牡丹长期发展，历久不衰。

在清代，甘肃大部分地区也有牡丹栽培，兰州、临夏、临洮一带为栽培中心。清末编纂的《甘肃新通志》曾有牡丹在甘肃"各州府都有，惟兰州较盛，五色具备"的记载。延安万花山，位于杜甫川内花源头村对面，盛产牡丹。清嘉靖修《延安府志》中记有"花源头产牡丹极多，樵者以之为薪"。附近群众有在农历四月初八到此赏花的习俗，已有一千多年的历史。

江南牡丹中有宁国牡丹和铜陵牡丹。据1936年编《宁国县志》载："宁国、蟠龙素产牡丹，以白、黄为贵……"关于铜陵牡丹，据《铜陵县志》载："仙牡丹长山石窦中，有白牡丹一株……

to the public's love for peony, Caozhou people's expertise, and its medicinal value, Caozhou peony endured quite a long prosperity.

Besides Caozhou, most places in Gansu Province also planted peony in the Qing Dynasty. Lanzhou, Linxia, Linyao were the centers there. *The New History of Gansu* written at the end the of the Qing Dynasty recorded that peony was planted in many places of Gansu and only Lanzhou had the most tree peonies with five colors of flowers. Wanhua Mountain, opposite Huayuantou Village and in Dufu Valley of Yan'an, Shaanxi Province abounds with peony flowers. *The History of Yan'an* complied during the Emperor Jiajing of the Qing Dynasty says that, "There are so many tree peonies near Hua Yuan Tou village that woodmen cut them as firewood." Every year on April 8th of the lunar calendar, people nearby go there and appreciate peony flowers. This activity has been held for more than one thousand years.

For regions in the south of the Yangtze River, Ningguo and Tongling were most famous for their peony. According to *The History of Ningguo* written in 1936, "Ningguo and Panlong has a long history of peony planting, and white and yellow peony flowers are valued most." As for Tongling peony, *The History of Tongling* recorded that, "There is a white tree peony in a stone hole of Changshan Mountain. Gorgeous and elegant, it is called Xian Mu Dan (peony from Heaven). Local people believed that it was planted by Ge Hong." Ge Hong is a chemist of the Jin Dynasty. Based on this story, it has grown for around 1600 years.

Since the establishment of People's Republic of China, peony planting gains new development and peony is still favored by Chinese people. Research on peony and related cultivation techniques have developed quickly. The planting area of peony in Heze, Shandong Province now is more than fifty thousand *mu* (more than 3300 hectares), with more than 600 species. Heze thus becomes the world's largest peony planting, appreciating and research center with the most species. Luoyang, with its various peony species and rich peony culture, remains the center of peony in China. In 2012, six new species, including Hei Tao Huang Hou (queen of spades) and Dong Li Yin Nan (east fence in silver south), developed by the technicians of Luoyang International Peony Garden, got certification from the authorized sector, adding the number of Luoyang peony species to 1036 in 2012 from 1030 in 2011.

An overview of peony history in China shows that the middle and lower reaches of the Yellow River are the main center of peony planting, with other places being sub-centers or major planting areas. Though the planting center changes with the shift of dynasties, it remains in the middle and lower

素艳绝丽。相传为葛洪所种。"葛洪为晋代人,按此传说,这株牡丹已有约1600年的历史。

中华人民共和国成立后,牡丹种植得以恢复和发展。牡丹依旧受到大家的喜爱,对牡丹的研究与栽培开发等技术也日益成熟。目前,山东菏泽牡丹栽培面积已有5万余亩,600多个品种,已成为世界上面积最大、品种最多的中国牡丹栽培、观赏、科研中心,堪称世界之最。而洛阳的牡丹与牡丹文化依然在民众心中保持着中心地位。2012年,由洛阳国际牡丹园培育的"黑桃皇后""东篱银南"等6个新品种正式通过有关部门鉴定,至此,洛阳牡丹由2011年的1030种增至1036种。

综观中国牡丹栽培的历史,形成了以黄河中下游为主要栽培中心,其他地区为次栽培中心或重要栽培地的格局。随着朝代的更迭,牡丹栽培中心亦有变换，但主要栽培中心始终位于黄河中下游地区。其转移过程为：洛阳（隋）—长安（唐）—洛阳（五代、宋）—亳州、曹州（明）—曹州（清）。这是中国牡丹品种群形成和发展的主线。除此之外，还有几个发展中心：一是长江三角洲、太湖周围及皖东南，二是四川盆地西北隅的成都、彭州，三是甘肃的兰州、临夏，四是广西的灌阳。

reaches of the Yellow River. From Luoyang (the Sui Dynasty), to Chang'an (the Tang Dynasty), to Luoyang (the Five Dynasties and Song Dynasty), Bozhou and Caozhou (the Ming Dynasty), and finally Caozhou (the Qing Dynasty), the middle and lower reaches of the Yellow River had always been the main areas for peony planting and new species development. Besides the main area, there are four sub-centers: the Yangtze River delta, Taihu Lake district and southeast of Anhui Province; Chengdu and Pengzhou on the northwest of Sichuan Basin; Lanzhou and Linxia in Gansu Province; and Guanyang in Guangxi.

2 牡丹花的神话传说
Myths and Legends of Peony

Native to China, peony has a long history of development and has been one of Chinese people's favorite flowers since ancient time. During the peony planting and appreciating, Chinese people made a lot of conjectures and guesses about its origin, development, change and breeding. As peony is regarded as the king of flowers and national flower for its elegance and beauty, people always relate it to royal families, flower faeries and faithful love. Legends on peony are also full of these romantic elements. They satisfy people's imagination on peony, the king of flowers.

牡丹是我国独有的花卉，历史悠久，在与人们的长期接触中产生了非常多的民间传说与神话故事。世人爱牡丹，对于其来源、发展、变迁、繁殖等有着诸多的臆想与猜测。另外，牡丹因其花王之姿、国花之态，总让人将她与帝王皇家、花神仙女、忠贞爱情等相联系，关于牡丹的传说，也充满了这些美艳高贵而又浪漫的元素。世人通过对这些传说的构筑，来满足自己对于花王牡丹的遐想。

一、人们关于牡丹起源与进化的猜想

（一）关于牡丹起源的传说

鹦哥救母。从前，在洛阳北邙山住着一对勤劳善良的夫妻。小两口男耕女织，恩恩爱爱，但有一样不顺心，成亲三年还没有孩子。有一天，小两口从一只凶猛的老鹰的爪下救下一只美丽的鹦鹉。鹦鹉得知小两口的心事后，从邙山仙人台上衔回来了灵芝草。妻子吃了灵芝草，不多久，生了个胖小子，取名叫鹦哥。鹦哥10岁那年，邙山上流行一种病，好多人染病卧床不起，爸爸不幸去世，妈妈也奄奄一息。鹦哥决心找到仙人台，挖来灵芝草为妈妈治病。他走呀，走呀，也不知趟过几条河，翻过几道岭，眼看走不动了，迎面遇到一位白胡子爷爷。白胡子爷爷问小鹦哥为啥出远门，鹦哥说要找灵芝草救妈妈。白胡子爷爷摇头说，你妈

1. Imagination on peony's origin and evolution

Legend on peony's origin

Yingge saves his mother. Once upon a time, there was a kind and hardworking couple living on Mangshan Mountain, north of Luoyang. With the husband working in the farm and wife weaving at home every day, they had everything they want except a baby. Having been married for three years, they still didn't have their child. One day, the couple saved a beautiful parrot from a fierce eagle. This lovely parrot knew the couple's worry, so it carried ganoderma from the celestial rock on Mangshan Mountain for them. Soon after the wife had the ganoderma, she gave birth to a baby, named as Yingge (parrot). When Yingge was ten years old, an infectious disease hit Mangshan Mountain. Many people were infected and had to stay in bed. Yingge's father died of the disease, leaving his dying wife and young son. Yingge therefore made up his mind to go to the celestial rock and find the ganoderma to save his mother. After he waded through countless rivers and climbed countless mountains, he came across an old man with long white beard when he could not walk any more. The old man asked Yingge why he had walked this far, and was answered that he wanted to find celestial ganoderma to save his mother. But the old man shook his head, saying that the ganoderma could not cure his mother's disease. He gave Yingge a stone and told him, "If you can grind the stone into a key, you may save your mother." With these words, the old man disappeared. Yingge then went to the river bank, found a big green stone and started to grind the stone the old man gave. Because of hard work, both his hands and knees bled. After three days and nights' work, the stone was finally ground into a key. Suddenly the old man appeared again. He praised Yingge and said, "There is an abode of immortals in the Heaven called Yao Chi. It is where the queen of heaven lives. The key can open the door of Yao Chi and you will find many grains of golden elixir there. One grain of them will save your mother's life." He then blew a wind to send Yingge to Heaven. Yingge opened the door with the key, found elixir in a calabash and took one grain out. When he was leaving, he remembered that people on Mangshan Mountain also needed his help, so he turned the calabash upside down, pouring all grains into his pockets. But it took some time and the queen of heaven soon found her elixir stolen. She hurriedly chased after Yingge. How could he run faster than her? When he was running anxiously, he suddenly noticed that the land underneath was Mangshan Mountain already. He then threw all the elixir there, speaking to himself, "Though I may be punished to death, people who found it can at least save their lives." Before long the queen of Heaven caught Yingge and was about to kill him, the old man appeared again, asking her to forgive Yingge. It turned out that the old man was the god of

得的是冷热病，灵芝草治不好。他交给鹦哥一块石头，说："你把这石头磨成钥匙，你妈的病才有指望。"说完，白胡子爷爷不见了。鹦哥来到河边，找块青石就磨开了石头。手磨出血来了，膝盖跪出血来了，这样三天三夜，石头终于磨成了钥匙。白胡子爷爷又出现了。他笑着夸赞小鹦哥一番，然后说道："天上有个地方叫瑶池，瑶池里住着一个神仙王母娘娘，这钥匙能打开瑶池的门，那里面放有救命神药金丹，一粒就可救你妈妈的命。"说完，他吹口仙气把鹦哥送到了天宫。鹦哥用石头钥匙打开了瑶池的门，找到了装着金丹的葫芦，倒出一粒金丹。他刚要出门，又想起邙山的乡亲们也需要金丹救命，便把葫芦倒了个底朝天，尽其衣兜装满金丹。也许是时间耽误太久，王母娘娘发现金丹被偷，急忙追来。鹦哥哪里能跑得过王母娘娘！正在焦急之时，忽从云缝间见地上已是邙山，鹦哥便不顾一切地把金丹全部撒下，心想：我大不了一死，但乡亲们谁拾到金丹，或可保住一命。王母娘娘抓住鹦哥，便要处死，白胡子爷爷突然又出现了。原来，他是南极仙翁神仙。南极仙翁向王母娘娘求情，保住了鹦哥的性命。仙翁又告诉鹦哥，你撒下的金丹会即刻长出一种奇花，可用它的根熬药治病。鹦哥回到邙山，果然见满山遍野都是鲜花。他把经历告诉了妈妈和乡亲，大家把花根刨出来熬药汤，喝了病立马好了。因这花是王母娘娘的金丹变的，人们便给这花取名"母丹"，叫着叫着人们便将此花叫做牡丹（在汉语中，"母丹"与"牡丹"同音）了。

（二）关于牡丹品种繁殖与栽培的传说

"刘师阁"。隋朝末年，在河南汝州的庙下镇东，居住着刘氏家族。刘家有一个美丽天真的少女，自幼琴棋书画，无所不通，

longevity. He told Yingge that the elixir he scattered had grown into golden flowers and their root, after boiled with water, can cure the disease. When Yingge was back, he saw golden flowers blooming all over the mountain. He told his mother and people his experience, and asked them to do what the god of longevity said. All the people got cured soon after they had the boiled roots. As the flower grows from the queen of the heaven's elixir, people called it "母丹"(Mu Dan, the queen's elixir). But as time went by, "母丹" was changed to "牡丹" (peony, the same pronunciation of "Mu Dan" in Chinese).

Legends on different peony species and peony breeding

Liu Shi Ge (Liu's Pavillion). There was a Liu family in the east of Miaoxia Town, Ruzhou, Henan Province in the end of the Sui Dynasty. Their daughter not only was beautiful and lovely, but also knew a lot about music, Chinese chess, calligraphy and painting, thus she was favored by all her relatives and neighbors. After her parents' death, she moved to Chang'an (today's Xi'an) with her brother, who was appointed as an official there. When the Sui Dynasty ended, her brother and sister-in-law passed away in succession, leaving her alone in the world. Having nowhere to go, she became a Buddhist nun and brought the white tree peony her families planted to the temple, showing her faith for Buddhism and wish for preserving her moral integrity. Under her good care, the peony grew tall and beautiful, with thousands of flowers blooming in spring. These flowers were as white as the beauty's skin and as crystal-clear as baby's face. All the people who saw it were amazed by its beauty and spoke highly of its elegance. Therefore, every April many Buddhism believers went to appreciate it and used the flower to show their sincerity towards Buddha. As it came from Liu family, it was named Liu Shi Ge (Liu's pavilion). Later this species was introduced to Tianpeng, Sichuan Province, Heze, Shandong Province and other places, gaining great popularity.

Dai Liu Huang (Bad Liu's yellow peony). Once upon a time, there was a young man named Liu Danting living near Luoyang. He had been fond of flowers and flower planting since childhood. Liking peony best, Liu planted many tree peonies around his house. However, as his peony was the best there, many naughty boys often picked his flowers. Quite

备受亲戚邻里的喜欢。随后父母相继过世，少女便随在长安做官的哥嫂来到长安定居。隋朝灭亡后，哥嫂相继谢世，独留她孤身一人，她无处可去，竟出家做了尼姑。出家时，少女将原来家院里亲手种植的白牡丹带到庵中，以表献身佛教、洁身自好之意。在她的精心培育下，白牡丹长得非常茂盛、美丽。一株之上开花千朵，花大盈尺，花色白并微带红晕，晶莹润泽，如美人肌肤、童子玉面。观者无不赞其美，颂其佳，故每逢四月，众多信女纷纷前来此庵拜佛观花，且以花献佛为乐，庵中香火愈旺。因此花出自"刘氏居之阁下"之手，故名为"刘氏阁"，又叫"刘师阁"。后来，此牡丹品种又传到四川天彭、山东菏泽等地，芳香远播。

"歹刘黄"。古时候，洛阳附近有一个后生，姓刘名丹亭。他自小爱花如痴，种花成癖，在百花之中，尤好牡丹，屋前屋后种了许多牡丹。然而正因为他花种得特别好，常遭顽童袭扰。他非常生气，每次凡被他捉住者，轻则被罚劳作一晌，重则被打板数下。因此，当地顽童便给他起了个绰号叫"歹刘"，并逐渐传开。有一年，他培育出一株黄金色的牡丹，其花色越过"姚黄"，众乡邻惊叹，富贵人家以金银相求。当时黄色的牡丹十分稀少，他便进行大量繁殖，一时远近争相购买，成为一种时尚。以后，人们将这种花命名为"歹刘黄"，这品名被载入书中，流传下来。

金黄牡丹。在云南省大理的洱海边，有座美丽的山，名叫点苍山。在这深山之中，生长着一种世界著名的金黄牡丹，不仅色如黄金，而且形似元宝，非常惹人喜欢。据当地的白族兄弟讲，它是由金子变成的。其来源有一段动人的故事。元朝末年，山中常闹土匪。一位当地的白族老汉以卖柴为生，一天进山砍柴遭土匪绑架，土匪放出风来，限

angry about this, every time Liu caught the pickers, he would ask them to work for him for a half day or spank them. The boys therefore called him Dai Liu (Bad Liu) and such name was gradually accepted by others. One year, he bred a new golden peony species which was even brighter than Yao Huang (Yao's yellow, another species famous for its yellow color). This astonished his neighbors and many rich men came to buy it with gold or sliver when hearing it. As there were few yellow peony species at that time, Liu enlarged its planting area and people nearby all bought the peony, forming a fashion. People called this peony Dai Liu Huang (Bad Liu's yellow peony). This name later was recorded in books and handed down to generations.

Golden Peony. There is a beautiful mountain named Diancang Mountain near Erhai of Dali, Yunnan Province. In the mountain grows a famous golden peony. Its flowers not only have gold color but also look like shoe-shaped gold ingot (an valuable currency in ancient China). According to local people, it is made of gold and there is a moving story about its origin. In the last years of the Yuan Dynasty, there were a lot of bandits. One day an old man who made a living by selling firewood was caught by these bandits when he was in the mountain. They said that his families must give them five kilograms of gold within three days, otherwise he would be killed. But the old man only had a young daughter, A Qing, who had nothing to give them. Hearing the news, A Qing was quite upset at first but she soon got an idea. On the third day, she brought a bag of golden stones and a sharp sword to see the bandits. When they saw the young girl, these bandits were very happy and did not take any precaution. She threw all the golden stones on the ground and they hurriedly ran towards the stones, fighting for their own share. At that moment, A Qing seized her opportunity and killed the leader. Seeing this, other bandits ran away like frightened birds. A Qing saved her father and in the place where she threw the golden stones grew golden peony.

2.Love Stories of Peony: Expressing love and fondness

Pocket Peony. There was an interesting custom in Miaoxia Town, Ruzhou, southeast of Luoyang: when two lovers were engaged, the girl should give her lover a small pocket embroidered with mandarin ducks as a love token. In the town lived a beautiful girl named Yunü. Eighteen years old, smart and dexterous, she had a gift in embroidery. The flowers she embroidered could even attract bees and butterflies. Such a good girl of course was

其家人三日之内带上黄金百两进山来赎，期限一过性命难保。老汉家中只有一个相依为命的独生女阿青，她闻讯后十分伤心。家中贫寒如洗，哪有金银？异常聪颖的她转念一想，有了主意。第三天，她只身带了一袋染了金色的石块和一把利剑上山。土匪们见是一年轻貌美的柔弱女子，眼都看直了，哪曾防备？她把金色的石块抛在地上，土匪们蜂拥来抢，她乘机一剑杀了土匪头目，其余人顿作鸟兽散，阿青救出了父亲。后来，就在她抛"金"之地，长出了金黄牡丹。

二、传情表意：牡丹花里的爱情传说

荷包牡丹。古时，在洛阳城东南的汝州庙下镇，有一个美妙的风俗习惯：男女青年一旦定亲，女方必须亲手给男的送去一个绣着鸳鸯的荷包作为定情信物。镇上有一位美丽的姑娘，名叫玉女。玉女芳龄十八，心灵手巧，天生聪慧，绣花织布技艺精湛，尤其是绣在荷包上的各种花卉图案，竟常招惹蜂蝶落在上面，可见其功夫之深。这么好的姑娘，提亲者自是踏破了门槛，但都被姑娘家人一一婉言谢绝。原来姑娘已有钟情的男子，家里也默认了。可惜，小伙在塞外充军已经两载，杳无音信，更不曾得到荷包。玉女日日盼，夜夜想，苦苦思念，便每月绣一个荷包聊表思念之情，并一一挂在窗前的牡丹枝上。久而久之，荷包形成了串，变成了人们所说的那种"荷包牡丹"了。

香玉和绛雪。崂山下清宫有株耐冬树，高两丈、大数十围，旁有一株牡丹高丈余，开时繁花似锦。胶州黄生在此读书，不觉恋上花仙香玉。一天晚上香玉含泪作别，说她将大祸临头。次日，即墨县蓝姓人来此游玩，见到院中白牡丹，即向人索求并将之挖走，黄生悟

courted by many young men. There were so many people coming to make a propose that the threshold of her house was stepped broken. But they were all turned down politely, because Yunü had been deeply in love with a young man and her family agreed on their relationship. But he was enlisted in the army and went to the west two years ago. Never sending a letter back, he could not get her pocket. Yunü missed him day and night. She embroidered a pocket every month to express her lovesickness and then hung them on the branches of tree peony near her window. As time passed, these pockets were connected to several strings and the peony was called Pocket Peony.

Xiangyu and Jiangxue. At the foot of Laoshan Mountain, there was a huge honeysuckle tree in the Purity Palace. It was two *zhang* (more than 6 meters) tall and too wide to be circled by dozens of persons with their hands joined together. Beside it was a tree peony, more than three meters tall and as beautiful as a painting when its flowers blossomed. It was named Xiangyu, and was actually a flower fairy. When Huang, a young man from Jiaozhou, Shandong came to study here, he fell in love with this beautiful peony without knowing its real identity. One day Huang dreamed that Xiangyu came to say good-bye with tears. She said that she would face an imminent disaster soon. The next day a man named Lan from Jimo came to visit the palace. When he saw the peony, he asked to take it away. Huang then realized that Xiangyu was a flower fairy and felt very sad about her leaving. Several days later, he heard that the peony withered. Grieving about her death, he composed fifty poems and went to the palace where she once lived every day. His behaviors moved Xiangyu's friend, Jiangxue. She told him that the god of flowers was greatly touched by his sincerity and had allowed Xiangyu to go back to the Purity Palace. Two days later, Xiangyu told Huang to find a grass named radix ampelopsis on Laoshan Mountain, dry it in the sun, pulverize it with a few sulfur, steep them in the water, and then use the mixed to water the place where the peony was. Huang did what she told and soon a new peony grew there. The next April, when peony flowers blossomed, Huang saw a small beauty standing on the pistil. It was Xiangyu. They got married and lived a happy life.

3.Legend of peony fairy: never forget others' help or yield to power

Empress Wu Angrily Banished Peony. Empress Wu, the only empress in Chinese history, once wrote a poem when she was admiring snow in imperial garden and got drunk, "Tomorrow I will visit the garden again. Do tell the god of spring at top speed: all flowers should bloom overnight, and do not wait for morning breeze." She then asked her maid to burn the scroll where the poem was written in the garden so that the god of spring could get the message. Hearing the poem,

到这香玉是牡丹仙子，很是惋惜。几天后，听说移走的牡丹枯死，黄生更是伤心，作诗50首，每日到牡丹穴旁凭吊。香玉的朋友绛雪很是感动，便告诉黄生，花神为其至情所感动，让香玉再回下清宫。两天后，香玉来见黄生，告诉他崂山上有一种白蔹草，挖来晒干碾碎，稍掺硫黄，浸泡于水中，每天到穴上浇洒一次，明年此日会来报答他的恩情。黄生依法去做，不久便长出一牡丹，次年4月花开，黄生见蕊中一小小美人飘然而来，竟是香玉。从此二人相亲相爱，生活幸福。

三、不畏强权感恩图报：牡丹花仙的神话传说

武则天怒贬牡丹。我国历史上唯一的一位女皇帝武则天于一年冬天至皇家上苑饮酒赏雪，酒后在白绢上写了一首五言诗："明朝游上苑，火速报春知。花须连夜发，莫待晓风吹。"写罢，她叫宫女拿到上苑焚烧，以报花神知晓。诏令焚

烧以后，吓坏了百花仙子。第二天，除了牡丹外，其余花都开了。武则天见牡丹未开，盛怒之下，将牡丹施以火刑，并贬出长安，发配洛阳。牡丹遭此劫难，体如焦炭，却根枝不散，在严寒凛冽中挺立依然，来年春风劲吹之时，花开更艳，被誉为"焦骨牡丹"。

青龙卧墨池。相传，曹州一棵修炼百年的红牡丹得到仙水沐浴后，竟然变成了一位红衣少女。天兵天将闻讯后来捉拿为之浇灌仙水触犯天条的小青龙。红衣少女为了救小青龙，飞到泰山墨池，把全身浸泡成黑色，把小青龙藏在自己的花心里。从此，曹州牡丹园里添了一种名贵牡丹——青龙卧墨池。

the fairy of flowers was almost frightened to death. The next morning, all flowers bloomed except peony. Noticing this, Empress Wu was in a towering rage. She demanded that peony should be burned and would never be planted in Chang'an again. It could only stay in Luoyang. After such disaster, peony's stem was burnt as black as coke, but it remained straight in chilly wind. The next spring, peony flowers were even brighter than before. People praised it as Coke Peony.

Cyan Dragon in Black Lake. There was a one-hundred-year-old red peony in Caozhou which after watered by celestial water, became a girl in red. Hearing these, troops in Heaven came to arrest the cyan dragon which watered the red peony. To save him, the girl flew to the black lake in Mountain Tai and dipped herself in the water until she became all black. She then hid the dragon in the heart of her flower so that he could not be found. Since then, Caozhou gained a new peony species called Cyan Dragon in Black Lake.

3 文学艺术中的牡丹花
Peony in Literature and Arts

Everyone loves beauty. As the national flower of China, peony receives more love and admiration than others. It is not only its beautiful appearance, but also its internal elegance and dignity that Chinese people love. For thousands of years, many poets and writers have written countless works to praise its beauty and express their love for it.

1.Peony in literature

Works related to peony can be found throughout history, from *The Books of Songs,* China's first collection of poems and songs, to *Luoyang Peony,* China's first works on the history, planting, species, and related customs of peony by Ouyang Xiu, and from Tang poems, Song iambic verse, Yuan drama,

爱美之心，人皆有之，而牡丹作为中国人心中的国花，更受爱戴。中国人赏牡丹，不仅赏其外在，更赞叹其神韵。中国人爱牡丹，不仅爱其形美，更爱其富丽端庄雍容大气的品格。千百年来，多少文人骚客为咏牡丹之美，为抒爱花之情，留下无数关于牡丹的文学艺术作品。

一、文学作品里的牡丹意蕴

从我国第一本诗歌总集《诗经》中对牡丹的只言片语的记载到欧阳修所著的关于地区牡丹的历史、栽培、品种以及风俗民情的我国第一部牡丹专著《洛阳牡丹记》，从唐诗、宋词、元曲、明清小说到现代诗词曲赋等文艺，都有不少关于牡丹的脍炙人口的作品。其中，有赞美牡丹之美的，如唐代刘禹锡的《赏牡丹》："庭前芍药妖无格，池上芙蕖净少情。唯有牡丹真国色，花开时节动京城。"有赞美牡丹高尚品格的，如清代潘韵的《咏白牡丹》："千红万紫斗芳春，羌独生成洁白身。似厌繁华存太素，甘抛富贵作清贫。"有描述与牡丹有关的社会活动的，如北宋苏轼的《吉祥寺赏牡丹》："人老簪花不自羞，花应羞上老人头。醉归扶路人应笑，十里珠帘半上钩。"唐朝白居易的《买花》："帝城春欲暮，喧喧车马度。共道牡丹时，相随买花去。"关于牡丹的文学作品，大多词句优美、寓意深刻，给人艺术美的享受，并从一定程度上反映了社会生活的另一侧面。

另外，自汉唐以来，还有不少关于牡丹的小说、戏曲流传于世。明清小说《镜花缘》《聊斋志异》

to modern literature. Some of them praise the beauty of peony, such as Liu Yuxi of the Tang Dynasty's *Appreciating Peony*, "The Chinese peony in the courtyard is too coquettish to have elegance, and the lotus in the lake is too clean to have emotions. Only peony has the national beauty, and even people in the capital are captured by its blossom." Some praise the nobility of peony, such as Pan Yun of the Qing Dynasty's *Ode to White Peony*, "So many red and purple flowers emulate each other in spring, and only you choose to remain white. Prefer purity to prosperity, and leave richness for poverty." Some described social activities related to peony: in *Appreciating Peony in Jixiang Temple*, Su Shi of the Song Dynasty wrote, "Though I am old now, I do not feel bashful of wearing a peony flower on my head. It is the peony that should feel bashful. When I was going home, I got drunk and leaned on the wall to walk. Seeing this, people nearby half opened their door, trying to hide their smile." Bai Juyi of the Tang Dynasty in *Buy Flower* wrote, "Though the spring is going to end in the capital, there are still many noisy sedans and horses on the road. They say that peony flowers are now in blossom, and they are going together to buy some home." Most works describing peony have beautiful verses and deep meaning, not only making readers enjoy the beauty of arts, but also reflecting some aspects of the society.

There are also many novels and dramas describing peony since the Han and Tang dynasties, such as *Flowers in the Mirror, Strange Tales from a Scholar's Studio,* and *Peony Pavillion* created during the

Ming and Qing dynasties. One that specially worth mentioning is *Peony Pavillion* by Tang Xianzu of the Ming Dynasty, which uses peony to praise romantic love and has moved many people. It tells a story that a girl named Du Liniang meets her lover Liu in her dream at the Peony Pavillion but the drop of a petal wakes her up. Since then she starts her pursuit for love with all her efforts. Her passion for love, just like peony's pursuit for ideal beauty rather than life, impresses many readers. Besides, many modern and contemporary treatises on peony have been published, including Yu Heng's *Caozhou Peony, Heze Peony,* and *Peony;* Li Jiayu's *Peony and Chinese Peony;* Wang Lianying's *China's Peony Cultivars;* Wang Gaochao's *Peony in China: Cultivation, Appreciation and Peony Culture;* Du Bingshen's *Selected Peony for Aesthetic Appreciation;* Ma Chengzhi's *Poems and Paintings on Peony and Chinese Peony,* etc..

2.Peony in paintings

Because of its beauty and elegance, peony is one of the major subjects in Chinese painting. Believing that to paint a subject, one needs to observe its appearance and then gets the image from his mind, Chinese painters usually use four basic techniques to paint peony: line drawing, fine brushwork, boneless painting and untrammeled painting.

等，明代汤显祖的《牡丹亭》，以牡丹歌颂至情至圣的浪漫主义，震撼人们的心灵。《牡丹亭》中，杜丽娘因游园赏春时萌动情思梦中与柳生在牡丹亭畔相会，怎奈一瓣落花惊醒春梦。丽娘从此开始对爱的不懈追求，这种青春的激情，一如牡丹"舍命不舍花"追求美丽理想境界的执着热烈，是扣人心弦的强烈情感。到现当代，也出现大量关于牡丹的文献和著作，如喻衡的《曹州牡丹》《菏泽牡丹》《牡丹花》、李嘉珏的《中国牡丹与芍药》、王连英的《中国牡丹品种图志》、王高潮的《中国牡丹：培育与鉴赏及文化渊源》、杜炳申的《艺用牡丹精粹》、马成志的《牡丹芍药题画诗》等。

二、绘画艺术里的牡丹形象

牡丹花国色天香，气韵天成，历来是中国画的重要题材之一。中国画家"外师造化，中得心源"，运用白描法、工笔法、没骨法和写意法四种基本技法描绘牡丹。晋代大画家顾恺之，曾于《洛神赋图卷》中画出了临风摇曳的牡丹与美丽妩媚的洛神在洛水边相伴。唐代牡丹兴盛，牡丹画也发展起来，画家边鸾，牡丹画作有《牡丹图》《孔雀牡丹图》，被时人评价为"妙得生意，不失润泽"。宋朝时，象征富贵的牡丹是院体画的重要素材，著名花鸟画家黄筌以双钩上彩法画牡丹，如《牡丹戏猫图》《牡丹鹁鸽图》等。元代的牡丹画以工笔为主，既继承南宋院体画画风又加以创新。明清则是牡丹画的辉煌时期，名家辈出，流派纷呈：有的厚重凝炼、古拙苍劲；有的缜密清丽，秀雅清润。其中吴昌硕所画牡丹格调高迈清爽。恽南田画牡丹大红大绿，凌跨明代画花卉名家，其没骨画法，为后人争相仿效。近代画家画牡丹，形式更加多样，或工笔或写意；风格各异。齐白石画牡丹，妙在似与不似之间，不重装饰重写意；张大千的牡丹画，特色鲜明。不论何种技法，都源自画者对国色天香的衷情，这种真情实感流于

Gu Kaizhi, a famous painter of the Jin Dynasty once depicted swaying peony flowers accompanying pretty goddess of Luo River on the river bank in *The Goddess of Luo River*. During the Tang Dynasty, because of people's love for peony, peony paintings also developed. Bian Luan's painting: *Peony*, and *Peacock and Peony*, were praised for "presenting peony's vitality creatively without losing its beauty". During the Song Dynasty, as the symbol of richness, peony became the main subject of imperial-court decorative paintings. Huang Quan, a famous flower-and-bird painter, used a technique named Outlining Before Coloring to paint peony. His works include *Peony with Playing Cat,* and *Peony and Pigeon.* In the Yuan Dynasty, peony painters mainly adopted fine brushwork, inheriting the style of the South Song Dynasty and also making some innovations. The Ming and Qing dynasties are the heyday of peony painting, with many famous painters and different schools appearing. Some of the paintings are concise and vigorous, while others are refined, clear and bright. Among them, Wu Changshuo's peony looks tall and refreshing and Yun Nantian's peony has bright red and green colors. Yun's paintings surpassed all works of the Ming Dynasty and his boneless painting technique was emulated by many descendants. Compared with ancient painters, modern painters chose more varied forms and techniques to depict peony, producing many styles. Qi Baishi's painting stood between resemblance and unlikeness, paying more attention to the will of painter than the ornament. Zhang Daqian's peony paintings have their own distinct features. All paintings, no matter which techniques are used, show painters' deep love towards peony. Their love, after flowing from their heart, to the brush and on the paper, enriches the aesthetic meaning of peony.

3.Peony in decorative arts

People's love towards peony not only can be found in their meticulous care in peony cultivation, but also in their various uses of peony image to decorate their life.

Floral designs of peony as decorations. One important way for Chinese people to show their fondness towards peony is redesigning the image of peony, and embroidering it on clothes, or painting it on chinaware, architecture and handicraft works. China being one of the four ancient civilizations in the world, many of its colorful textiles, dyeing cloths, and embroideries were transported to Europe, Africa and other Asian countries through Silk Road in history. One of the major floral designs these goods usually had was peony. Modern and contemporary designers also choose peony as a main theme in clothes design and fashion show. While inheriting traditional style, they use fine brushwork as main painting technique and choose red as ground color to show peony's elegance and beauty. Furthermore, peony is also an important subject for decoration of china, which enjoys high reputation both home and abroad for its unique shape, combination of aesthetic and practicability,

笔尖，展于纸上，丰富了牡丹的审美意境。

三、装饰艺术里的牡丹美学

世人对牡丹的喜爱，不仅表现为对其悉心栽培与呵护，更将牡丹形态通过各种巧妙的方式装点于自己生活中的方方面面。

通过花纹图案形式的装饰。 将牡丹形象根据主题进行临摹或抽象再经设计加工之后运用于服饰、瓷器、建筑和手工艺品上，是我国勤劳智慧的人民表达对牡丹喜爱之情的另一种重要方式。我国是世界四大文明古国之一，历代的花团锦簇的纺织品、五彩缤纷的印染品、绚丽多彩的刺绣品，就通过"丝绸之路"，传到欧亚非各国，牡丹花纹是其中的花纹图案的主体之一。近现代仍承袭传统，设计师在以牡丹图案为主体的服装设计、服装表演上，以工笔技法，红为底色，衬托大朵牡丹花，展现其高贵大方、雍容华丽的气质。中国瓷器以其独特的造型艺术、加工工艺和装饰图案，集观赏性与实用性于一身，享誉海内外。瓷器中人们以人物、山水、花鸟等作为装饰内容，牡丹是其中重要题材之一，江西的青花缠枝牡丹纹梅瓶、北京的剔红双龙牡丹山石纹盆、洛阳的唐三彩牡丹尊和牡丹枕等是其代表。在中国的民间建筑、宫殿建筑和手工艺品上，也都有牡丹雕刻装饰，既有立体感又有绘画的韵味。在全国各地，以牡丹为主体的木雕、石雕或刻石也为数不少，如明代的"牡丹童子格扇门花心"、清代的"四季花卉格扇门花心"等。

　　通过插花等实物方式的装饰。 插花、盆景等实物方式的装饰主要运用于室内，通过此种方式可将牡丹赏花活动从室外搬到室内。牡丹插花是中国传统插花艺术的精髓之一，早在唐代牡丹插花已十分流行，并达兴盛。它主要

processing techniques and decorative design. Other subjects for decoration include figures, landscape, flowers and birds. Famous china works with peony image are Blue and White Plum Blossom Vase with Interlocking Flowers made in Jiangxi Province, Red Pot with Two Dragons, Peony Flowers and Landscape from Beijing, and tri-colored glazed wine goblet and pillow with peony design of the Tang Dynasty in Luoyang. Peony can be found in folk architecture, palace buildings and handicraft works as well, which is a visual feast but also has the charm of painting. Wood-carvings and stone carvings with peony are all over China, such as Partition Door with Peony and Kids of the Ming Dynasty and Partition Door with Four Seasons' Flowers of the Qing Dynasty.

Peony flowers as decorations. Decorations like flower arrangement and bonsai are mainly placed indoors, enabling people to appreciate flowers in the house. Peony flower arrangement is one of the essences of Chinese flower arrangement art and has been quite popular since the early Tang Dynasty. Usually put in a disc or a vase, it at first was placed in front of Buddha in temples. Later royal families and ordinary people use it as a decoration. The basic principle of peony flower arrangement is "learning from nature and better than nature." As peony flowers are large and bright, the flower arrangement should be simple instead of complex, so as to achieve man-made natural beauty. Besides, peony flower arrangement pays great attention to the whole artistic effect, the meaning conveyed through flower arrangement and the demonstration of peony culture. The commonly used methods of naming a decoration to show its meaning are homophony, synonym and rhythm, such as putting peony in a vase to show richness and peace, (peony is the symbol of richness and the Chinese pronunciation of vase is the same as that of peace) or using the combination of Magnolia heptapeta, Malus spectabilis and peony to convey jade's nobleness, magnificence, and richness (Magnolia heptapeta's first Chinese character is the same of jade and Malus spectabilis' second character is the same of magnificence). Large and bright, peony flowers are suitable for large and medium-sized works to decorate hall, reading room, meeting room and living room. Having been favored by Chinese people since ancient times, peony flower arrangement will receive more attention and even play a big role worldwide, with China promoting traditional culture and national spirit.

以牡丹为花材作盘花和瓶供，使用范围从佛前供花扩展到宫廷和民间。牡丹插花首先要遵循"源于自然、高于自然"的基本原则。牡丹花大、色彩突出，因此构图宜简不宜繁，达到"虽由人作，宛自天开的境界"。其次，牡丹插花追求整体艺术效果，注意内涵和意境，体现花材的寓意和象征，并运用谐音、谐意手法表达作品的"花外之意"，更强调插花作品的意象美、韵律美。如将牡丹花插于瓶中寓意"富贵平安"，还有用玉兰、牡丹、海棠的组合，寓意"玉堂富贵"。牡丹花体量较大，花色艳丽，可作中型、大型插花作品，装饰效果强，适于布置在厅堂、会议室、书房、居室等处。牡丹插花深受人们的喜爱，在提倡中国传统文化、弘扬民族精神的今天，牡丹插花将受到国人的推崇与重视，并在国际插花的舞台上大放异彩。

4 牡丹与人们的生活
Peony and People's Life

牡丹在我国有着广泛的群众基础，在人民的日常生活中随处可见牡丹的身影。

一、以牡丹入馔

牡丹花的食用从我国古代就已经开始了。最早除了将牡丹入药，就是将牡丹做饼。相传牡丹饼是由武则天发明的。据《隋唐佳话录》载，有一年花朝节适逢牡丹盛开，她率宫女游园观花，看着争奇斗艳的花儿，突发奇想，命令宫女采下大量的各色花朵，回宫按她的设计，和米捣碎，蒸制成糕，即名"百花糕"。她用这香

Peony is quite popular in China and can be found everywhere in people's life.

1.Peony as food

Using peony flowers to make food started in ancient China. Besides being a medicinal material, peony flowers can also be used to make pancakes. It is said that the peony pancake was invented by Empress Wu. According to *The Anecdotes of Sui and Tang Dynasties:* during the Huazhao (flower blossom) Festival when peony flowers bloomed, Empress Wu went to imperial garden to appreciate colorful flowers with her maids. It suddenly occurred to her that these petals might be used to make food, so she asked her servants to pick many petals, mash them with rice to make cakes and then steam them. These cakes tasted delicious and were named Flower Cake. They were also called Peony Cake or Peony Pancake. Wu later gave away these cakes to her ministers to have a taste. During the Sui and Tang dynasties, Luoyang peony was introduced to Japan because of the frequent communications between China and Japan. Painters in Japan drew beautiful and elegant peony flower images on the wall of Nara's Kasuga Grand Shrine, which was regarded as a national treasure by Japanese people. The recipe of Peony Cake was also introduced to Japan at that time. After more than one thousand years, it is still very popular among Japanese people.

In the Five Dynasties, peony was used not only to make cakes but also imperial cuisine. According to *Fu Zhai Man Lu*（*Works Written in Study Fu*）, which was recorded in Volume 32, *Guang Qun Fang Pu (Collection of Plants),* "Li Hao, the minister of courtesy of the Later Shu Dynasty, once gave away several branches of peony and Xingping Cake to his friends, saying that, 'After the petals withered, fry them in shallow oil and then have a taste.' " *Zun Sheng Ba Jian* (*Eight Ways for Longevity*) of the Ming Dynasty says, "The fresh peony petals can also be fried." and *Yang Xiao Lu (Book on Diet)* of the Qing Dynasty says, "Peony petals can be eaten after boiled in water, soaked in honey or boiled in meat soup."

Current well-known peony cuisine include Petal Salad, and Fried Petals with Fillet. Petal Salad often chooses white or pink petals that taste less bitter, and then mixes them with mayonnaise. Its specific

糯可口的点心作为礼品分别赏赐群臣，故牡丹饼又称百花糕、牡丹糕。隋、唐两代中日交往频繁，洛阳牡丹传至日本，日本的画师把富丽端庄的中国牡丹彩绘在奈良"春日神社"的墙壁上，被日本人民奉若至宝。牡丹饼的制作也从洛阳传到日本，至今相延千余年，牡丹饼仍风行于日本民间。

至五代时期，牡丹不仅能做饼，还用于做宫廷菜。据《广群芳谱》卷三十二引《复斋漫录》云："孟蜀时，礼部尚书李昊每将牡丹花数枝分遗朋友。以兴平酥同赠，曰：'俟花凋谢，即以酥煎食之'。"明代《遵生八笺》上记载"牡丹新落瓣亦可煎食"。清朝《养小录》"牡丹花瓣，汤焯可，蜜浸可，肉汁烩亦可"。

现在比较有名的牡丹花菜肴有凉拌牡丹花和牡丹花里脊丝。凉拌牡丹花多选用涩味较少的白色或粉色花为原料并配以蛋黄酱等。制法是先将花瓣放在烧热的苏打水中焯一下，用水漂净，然后加入蛋黄酱等拌匀即可。还可以在做好的成菜上再点缀上一两片颜色鲜艳的牡丹花瓣，以增加整体菜品的色彩与层次。凉拌牡丹花看起来赏心悦目，吃起来清清淡淡，十分爽口。做牡丹花里脊丝的原料有牡丹花、猪里脊肉、鸡蛋、鸡汤、猪油、精盐、味精、湿淀粉、料酒等。先将牡丹花洗净去蕊并切成丝，里脊肉也切细丝，用盐、味精、鸡蛋清、湿淀粉拌匀上浆。取鸡汤、味精、酱油、料酒各少许兑成汁。炒勺烧热放入猪油，烧至五成熟时放入肉丝，炒散后烹入先调好的汁，待汁收浓时，放入切好的牡丹花丝，快速翻炒盛入盘内即可。这道菜的特点是味美清香，肉质鲜嫩。

二、以牡丹入茶

饮茶是我国的一个传统习俗，我国古时人们就有将牡丹花瓣洗净后加入茶中一起饮用的习惯，

procedure is as follows: boil peony petals in soda water for several seconds, rinse them, and then add some mayonnaise. One or two bright petals may also be added on the top to create more layers and make it better looking. The Peony Salad looks enjoyable and is very tasty. As for Fried Petals with Fillet, its ingredients include peony petals, fillet of pork, eggs, chicken stock, lard, salt, monosodium glutamate, starch mixed with water, and cooking wine. The procedure is: first, wash the petals and cut them into shreds. Second, cut the fillet into shreds and mix them with salt, monosodium glutamate, egg white and starch mixed with water. Third, add some monosodium glutamate, soy sauce and cooking wine in the chicken stock. Fourth, after the pan is heated, add lard and when the lard is half melted, add the shreds of fillet. Fifth, stir the shreds of fillet several times and add the chicken stock. Sixth, when the soup becomes denser, add petals and after quickly stir-frying the dish a few seconds, put it on the plate. It tastes delicate and the meat is quite tender.

2. Peony as tea

Drinking tea is one of the Chinese traditions. Since ancient times, Chinese people have added clean peony petals into the tea, to add the fragrance of peony and make use of its medicinal value.

According to *The Compendium of Materia Medica,* adding peony petals into tea and long-time peony tea drinking can prolong one's life. Now peony healthy tea is made by mixing peony petals with green tea leaves. It has 13 amino acids, vitamin, micro-elements, macro-elements and other natural elements.

3.Peony for bath

Peony can also be used for daily bath and it is called Peony Bath. By picking two or three peony flowers and floating them on the water, the person who bathes there will be surrounded by fragrance, feeling relaxed, improving blood circulation and even being able to take a nap.

4.Peony in music

There is a folk song named "Bian Hua Lan" (weaving the basket of flowers) in Henan Province, "Weave, weave, weave a basket. Weave a basket and go to the South Mountain. There are many red peony flowers on the mountain. Every flower is bright

不仅能使茶香中更多一缕牡丹清香，也能将牡丹的药用价值体现出来。《本草纲目》中指出，"茶中加入牡丹花瓣，久饮可延年益寿"。而在现代社会里，也已推出了牡丹保健茶，用绿茶为载体精制而成，含有13种氨基酸、维生素、微量元素、常量元素等天然成分。

三、以牡丹入浴

牡丹还可用于日常生活沐浴，被称为"牡丹浴"。将盛开的牡丹花剪下两三朵，漂浮在浴池之上，花瓣和雄蕊渐渐在水中散开，沐浴其中的人被花香包围，有助于身心放松，起到活血舒筋，帮助睡眠的作用。

四、以牡丹入歌

河南民歌《编花篮》："编，编，编花篮，编个花篮上南山，南山开满红牡丹，朵朵花儿开得艳……"这优美动听的歌曲，常激发人们无限的激情。现代歌曲赞美牡丹的也不少，电影《红牡丹》中插曲《牡丹之歌》，由蒋大为独唱，赞颂了牡丹的品格，概括了牡丹的特性，给人以蓬勃向上的激情。菏泽国际牡丹花会会歌《天下第一香》，歌曲甜美、轻盈，歌颂了曹州牡丹的芬芳："人说牡丹是天香，曹州的天香更芬芳，富贵花呀幸福花，织成彩云和霞光……四海盛赞曹州第一香，天下第一香。"

and beautiful..." This dulcet melody often inspires people's love for peony. Many modern songs also praise the beauty of peony. For example, *Song of Peony* by Jiang Dawei in the movie *Red Peony*, speaks highly of peony's character, touching many people's heart. And *First Fragrance*, theme song of Heze International Peony Festival, compliments Caozhou peony's fragrance with sweet and light-hearted melody, "People often say that peony's fragrance comes from Heaven. Caozhou's peony has the first fragrance. It has the flower of richness and happiness. It forms the rainbow and roseate clouds on earth...everyone says Caozhou has the first fragrance, the first fragrance."

5 从国内到国外：中华民族最美的容颜

From China to Abroad: the Most Beautiful Representative of Chinese People

Native to China, peony has formed its own culture, as part of Chinese civilization during thousands of years' evolution and cultivation. With its elegant beauty and unswerving will, it has been titled as the king of flowers several times since the Tang Dynasty. In 1959, when Premier Zhou Enlai visited Luoyang, he said, "Gorgeous and elegant peony is the symbol of China's richness and prosperity. We should restore peony planting and promote its development as soon as possible." For Chinese people, peony is the most beautiful representative of Chinese culture and spirit.

牡丹作为我国独有的原生花木，在其数千年的自然生长和两千多年的人工栽培历史中，形成了与华夏文明息息相关的牡丹文化，有华贵大气之形，又有坚毅刚强之骨。唐宋明清时期，牡丹数度被正式冠以"花魁""国花"之称。1959年，周恩来总理到洛阳视察时曾说："牡丹雍容华贵、富丽堂皇，是我们中华民族兴旺发达、繁荣昌盛的象征，要赶快促其恢复、发展、繁荣。"而在人们的心目中，牡丹早已是最能代表中华民族美好文化与传统精神的"最美容颜"。

随着牡丹被其他国家的引进与广泛栽培、繁殖，牡丹也越来越受到世界各国人民的喜爱。目前日本、法国、英国、美国、意大利、澳大利亚、新加坡、朝鲜、荷兰、加拿大等20多个国家均有牡丹栽培。其中以日、法、英、美等国的牡丹园艺品种和栽培数量为最多。公元724－749年，中国牡丹进入日本，据说是由空海和尚带去的。1330—1851年，法国对引进的中国牡丹进行大量繁育，培育出许多园艺品种。1656年，荷兰东鯿公司将牡丹引入荷兰，1789年英国丘园引进牡丹，从而使中国牡丹在欧洲传播开来，园艺品种有100多个。1880年，法国人对中国的野生黄牡丹进行育种，于1980年选育出一批黄色系品种，后来传入日本等国。美国于1820－1830年才从中国引进中国牡丹品种和野生种，后来培育出一种黑色花牡丹品种。在美国，许多国家森林公园里均栽有牡丹和芍药。英国丘园是收集世界牡丹品种

With peony being introduced to and planted in more and more countries, it becomes more and more popular in the world. Currently more than twenty countries have planted peony, including Japan, France, Great Britain, U.S., Italy, Australia, Singapore, DPRK, Holland and Canada. Among them, Japan, France, Great Britain, and U.S. have the most species and peonies. Peony was introduced to Japan during 724 to 749. It is said that it was Monk Kong Hai (a famous Japanese monk who after studying Buddhism in China during the Tang Dynasty, made a great contribution to the Buddhism development in Japan) who took peony to Japan. Frenchmen began to plant peony in large areas and bred many new species during 1330 to 1851. Dutch East India Company introduced peony to Holland in 1656, and Kew Gardens of Great Britain began to plant peony in 1789, promoting the spread of peony in Europe and increasing the number of species there to more than one hundred. By developing China's wild yellow peony species introduced in 1880, Frenchmen successfully bred a new series in 1980. Later, these species were introduced to Japan and other countries. America did not begin to plant peony until 1820 to 1830 and people there developed a black peony species. Now many national forest parks in America have peony and Chinese peony. Kew Gardens of Great Britain is one of the gardens that have the most peony species in the world, including many ancient ones coming from China and a lot of new ones developed by different countries.

Japan has the world's second largest planting area and number of tree peonies following China. Though the national flower of Japan is sakura, Japanese people are very fond of peony under the long-time influence of Chinese culture. Peony is planted in many place in Japan, such as Tokyo, Hasedera Temple and Sekkoji-Temple in Nara, Sukagawa, Okayama, peony garden for Master Nishii, Chiba University, and Shimane. Peony species in Japan totals more than three hundred, including Golden Pavilion, Golden King, Golden Sun, The King of Flowers, Sun, Hatsushima, Jade-white Lion, Minister of Flower, Fuji-no-mine, Kamata, Yachiyo and Sunset. According to Somei Takahiro's *Peony and Chinese Peony,* there are 312 peony species in Japan and 211 of them are developed by Japanese people. The one most worth mentioning is Cold Peony which can blossom in winter. It once shocked horticultural experts worldwide. Besides, the peony festival held in Daikon Island, Matsue every year is very popular in Japan.

较多的专类园之一，包括中国的许多古老品种和当今世界各国新育出的众多园艺品种。

日本是海外牡丹栽培面积最广、数量最多的国家。虽然日本的国花是樱花，但由于长期受到中国文化的深远影响，日本人对牡丹也十分珍爱。在日本众多的城镇中都普遍种植着牡丹，如东京的阿部牡丹园、奈良的长谷寺与石光寺、须贺川牡丹园、冈山牡丹园、新西井大师牡丹园、千叶大学园艺学部牡丹园、岛根中国牡丹园等。园艺品种有300多个，有金阁、金帝、金幌、金阳、花王、太阳、初岛、白玉狮子、花大臣、富士之峰、镰田藤、八千代子、日暮等。据染井孝熙著《牡丹与芍药》一书记载：日本现有牡丹品种312种，其中日本的改良种有211种，尤以日本培育出冬季开花的"寒牡丹"惊动世界园艺界。日本松江市每年举办的松江大根岛牡丹节，也非常受人欢迎。

综观牡丹与牡丹文化的形成与发展，可发现牡丹受人们喜爱的原因，主要有三点：

第一，牡丹是国家繁荣昌盛的象征。牡丹花开时节，繁花似锦，灿烂辉煌。在大唐盛世，全国上下无不为之倾倒，牡丹花季成了长安、洛阳的狂欢节。自唐宋以来，牡丹成为吉祥幸福、繁荣昌盛的象征，并得以世代延续下来。今天，牡丹的这一文化象征意义又被赋予了新的含义，因为她非常贴切地代表了改革开放的中国国泰民安、前程似锦的美好形象，具有鲜明的时代特征，表达了全国各族人民共同的理想和愿望。

An overview of peony and peony culture's development can explain why peony is so popular. There are three reasons for it.

First, peony is the symbol of national prosperity. During the Tang Dynasty, magnificent and gorgeous peony flowers captured everyone's heart and the blossom season of peony was time of carnivals for people in Chang'an and Luoyang. Since then, peony has been regarded as the symbol of happiness and prosperity. Today, the cultural meaning of peony has been enriched, for it represents the common wish of people of all nationalities in China, the promising image and prosperity of China since the reform and opening-up policy, and happy life of Chinese people.

Second, peony stands for people's wish and pursuit of richness. Its bright colors and large flowers make people relate it to richness. Since the Song Dynasty, peony has been called the flower of richness and was painted in many paintings and handcraft works to represent richness. Its different combinations with birds, landscape and other flowers imply various meanings besides richness.

Third, peony is upright and never yields to power. People's love for peony attaches it with Chinese spirit and noble character. There are two stories that show peony's nobility. One is that when Empress Wu went to imperial garden to admire snow, she was in high spirits, so she demanded that all flowers should blossom overnight. Being afraid of her power, all flowers were forced to bloom except peony. Because of it, Empress Wu angrily banished peony to Luoyang. The other is recorded in the novel *Old Man Comes Across Flower Fairy*. When a group of villains were trying to destroy flowers and forcibly seize a garden, it was peony fairy who brought flowers back to life and punished the villains. Therefore, people always speak highly of its braveness. Though regarded as the flower of richness, peony is not the flower in greenhouse.

第二，牡丹代表了人们对富裕生活的期盼与追求。牡丹花姹紫嫣红，富丽堂皇，从气质上给人以富贵之感。自宋以来，牡丹即被称为"富贵花"。在历代绘画及各种工艺美术作品中，牡丹作为富贵的象征，与其他花鸟、山石的不同组合，就表现出与富贵结合在一起的不同的寓意。

第三，牡丹有着劲骨刚心、不畏权贵的高风亮节。人们喜爱牡丹，赋予了牡丹能代表中华民族精神力量的优秀品格。武则天冬日游园，一时兴至，竟下令百花限时开放，百花慑于权势，不得不开，独牡丹没有按时开花，而被武则天下令放火烧之，贬出长安。在《秋翁遇仙记》中，一伙恶奴毁花霸园，是牡丹仙子及时赶来救活了被毁坏的牡丹花，严惩了暴徒。牡丹这种不畏权贵和恶势力的精神，备受称赞。作为"富贵花"，牡丹并不娇嫩脆弱，她原来生长在莽莽群山中，近代因为森林面积日渐缩小，滥挖药材，以至野牡丹只能在悬崖峭壁上顽强生长。在黄土高原干旱贫瘠的土地上，她仍然开出绚丽的花朵。

It originally grew in mountains and now due to deforestation, some wild peonies still manage to live on cliffs. Even in the dry and barren Loess Plateau, they still have bright flowers.

第二章

牡丹花都洛阳

　　尽管我国大多数地方都种植牡丹，很多城市也因牡丹而名噪一时，但能称为牡丹花都的唯有洛阳。洛阳不仅气候适宜、土壤肥沃，更因十三朝古都而使城有贵气。帝都繁华，人民安居乐业，具有较为丰富的文化生活和较高的文化品位。只有此种深厚的文化背景才能孕育出更具魅力的牡丹文化，将牡丹与牡丹文化推向更高层次的境界。一方水土养一方人，一方水土也养一方花，牡丹因洛阳更增气度与神韵，难怪欧阳修称"洛阳牡丹甲天下"。

Chapter Two

The Capital of Peony: Luoyang

Though most places in China planted peony and many cities are famous for their peonies, the only capital of peony is Luoyang. It not only has suitable climate and fecund soil, but also rich culture as the capital of thirteen dynasties. Luoyang people's prosperous and happy life, their good taste and rich culture breed charming peony culture and promote peony and its culture to a higher level. Each place has its own way of supporting its inhabitants and each place has its own way of supporting its flowers, too. Because of Luoyang, peony gains more charm and elegance. No wonder Ouyang Xiu said that "Luoyang peony is the best in China."

1 优越的自然生态环境
Favorable Natural Environment

Luoyang is in the west of Henan Province, from 111°8′ to 112°59′E and 33°35′ to 35°05′N. On the east part of Eurasian Continental Bridge, it stretches across the north and south banks of the Yellow River in the middle reaches, and as the middle part of China, it is also nicknamed as the belly of China.

洛阳，位于河南省西部，地处东经111°8′—112°59′、北纬33°35′—35°05′，位于亚欧大陆桥东段，横跨黄河中游南北两岸，"居天下之中"，素有"九州腹地"之称。

洛阳地理条件优越。它位于暖温带南缘向北亚热带过渡地带，属暖温带大陆性季风气候和亚热带季风气候，四季分明，气候宜人。年平均气温约15°C，极端最高气温40.4°C，极端最低气温零下20.2°C。降雨量约630毫米，其中南部山区有1200毫米以上。东邻郑州，西接三门峡，北跨黄河与焦作接壤，南与平顶山、南阳相连。东西长约179千米，南北宽约168千米。洛阳地势西高东低。境内山川丘陵交错，地形错综复杂，其中山区占45.51%，丘陵占40.73%，平原占13.8%，周围有郁山、邙山、青要山、荆紫山、周山、樱山、龙门山、香山、万安山、首阳山、黛眉山、嵩山等十多座山；境内河渠密布，分属黄河、淮河、长江三大水系，黄河、洛河、伊河、清河、磁河、铁滦河、涧河、瀍河等十余条河蜿蜒其间，有"四面环山、六水并流、八关都邑、十省通衢"之称。由

Luoyang has very favorable geological conditions. It is located on the transitional zone from warm temperate zone to subtropical zone. It has temperate continental monsoon climate and subtropical monsoon climate, with four distinct seasons and pleasant weather. The annual average temperature there is about 15 degrees Celsius, with the maximum temperature reaching 40.4 degrees Celsius and the minimum temperature -20.2 degrees Celsius. The average annual precipitation of Luoyang is around 630 millimeters with the south mountain having the most, more than 1200 millimeters. Its east is Zhengzhou and west is Sanmenxia. On the north Luoyang is connected to Jiaozuo by the Yellow River and on the south it is next to Pingding Mountain and Nanyang. The total area of Luoyang is about 179 kilometers long and 168 kilometers wide, with its west higher than the east. There are many mountains and hills in Luoyang, forming an uneven terrain. Its mountainous areas account for 45.51% of the total, hills for 40.73% and plains for 13.8%. Mountains there include Yushan Mountain, Mangshang Mountain, Qingyao Mountain, Jinzi Mountain, Zhoushan Mountain, Yingshan Mountain, Longmen Mountain, Xiangshan Mountain, Wan' an Mountain, Shouyang Mountain, Daimei Mountain and Mountain Song. Many tributaries of the Yellow River, the Huai River and the Yangtze River flow in Luoyang: the Yellow River, the Luo River, the Yi River, the Qing River, the Ci River, the Tieluan River, the Jian River, the Chan River, etc.. Therefore, Luoyang is surrounded by mountains in four directions and flown by plenty of rivers, being the traffic center of eight cities and ten provinces. Located in the middle of the central plains, Luoyang has Qinling Mountains to its west, Mountain Song to its east, Taihang Mountain and the Yellow River to its north, and Funiu Mountain to its south. Surrounded by mountains and rivers, Luoyang's location is very critical in China.

It is said that Luoyang is the most suitable place for peony. Those growing well in Luoyang, would grow smaller and smaller flowers once moved to other places, while those looking ordinary in other places would become luxuriant and grow brighter and brighter flowers once moved to Luoyang. Though this is a bit exaggerated, many gardeners do believe that Luoyang's climate and environment is very suitable for peony planting. There is an old saying that, "To plant peony well, you need the soil of Luoyang." Luoyang indeed, is the heaven for peony.

Situated among three rivers, Luoyang has been a good place to live since ancient times. Its climate is basically in accordance with China's 24 solar terms and has four distinct seasons, fitting the growth cycle of peony. The bud of peony begins to sprout and grow in the inception of spring. At that time, the average temperature of Luoyang is above 0 degree Celsius, offering a warm environment for

于洛阳地处中原，山川纵横，西依秦岭，出函谷是关中秦川，东临嵩岳；北靠太行且有黄河之险，南望伏牛，有宛叶之饶，所以"河山拱戴，形势甲于天下"。

有人称洛阳是最适合牡丹生长的地方，把原本在洛阳长得好好的牡丹移植到外地，就会慢慢退化，连花朵都会越开越小。而外地本来品相一般的牡丹移栽到了洛阳，一下就变枝繁叶茂，花也越开越娇艳。这种说法虽然有些夸张，但确实不少园林工作者都称洛阳的水土非常适宜种植牡丹。古人云："种植好牡丹，必取洛阳土。"洛阳确实是牡丹的天堂。

"洛阳居三河间，古善地。"其气候基本与我国"二十四节气"同步，四季分明，很符合牡丹的生长周期。"立春"时节，牡丹的幼芽开始膨大，并逐渐绽裂，而这时洛阳的平均气温已回升到0°C以上，适宜牡丹发芽。"谷雨"时节，洛阳气温稳定在17°C左右，牡丹自然进入开花期。洛阳冬季没有东北寒冷，夏季没有南方湿热，有利于牡丹的冬眠、越夏。

河洛地区有黄河、洛河、伊河等众多河流，由于它们的共同冲积，形成了洛阳盆地。洛阳盆地土地肥沃，且黏性较大，这对相对喜爱稍显干旱而怕涝的牡丹生长十分有利。

2004年4月，河南省地质调查院和洛阳市地矿局公布了一项科研成果，经过对560平方千米土壤的考察研究，发现洛阳一带土壤的各种微量元素，特别是锰、铜、锌、钼元素明显高出其他地区，其中锰的有效含量是其他地区平均含量的20多倍。这些微量元素能有效促进植物细胞生长，促进叶绿素、糖类、酶类的合成及花蕾的形成。洛阳土壤微量元素含量如此丰富，在于伊洛流域广泛分布着

the sprouting. Peony flowers begin blooming during Grain Rain (around April 19th to April 21st), when the temperature of Luoyang stays steadily around 17 degrees Celsius. As Luoyang's winter is not as cold as that in the northeast and its summer is not as hot as that in the south, peony growth does not encounter many difficulties in winter and summer.

There are many rivers flowing by Heluo district (the district between the Yellow River and the Luo River, including Luoyang, Zhengzhou and other cities), such as the Yellow River, the Luo River, and the Yi River. Their alluviation forms Luoyang basin. Its fertile and sticky soil is very favorable to peony growth which prefers dry soil to waterlogging.

In April 2004, Henan Geological Survey Institute and Luoyang Mining Bureau published their findings based on the research of 560 square kilometers' land. They found that the quantity of microelements in the soil of Luoyang is larger than that of other areas, especially in terms of manganese, copper, zinc and molybdenum. The effective quantity of manganese in the soil of Luoyang is about twenty times the average quantity of other areas. These microelements can effectively promote the growth of plant cell, accelerate the synthesis of chlorophyll, saccharides and enzymes, and improve the development of flower bud. Such high quantity of microelements is created by the weathering, alluviation and transportation of ancient volcanics distributed widely on the river basin of the Yi River and the Luo River. This explains why Luoyang is suitable for crop planting, especially flower planting. Seen from this perspective, the old saying that "To plant peony well, you need the soil of Luoyang" is indeed true and Ouyang Xiu's "Luoyang has the best peony in China" is not an empty sentence or flattery.

古老的火山岩，经过亿万年的风化、冲积、搬运，形成了洛阳适宜农作物种植尤其是花卉种植的特色。由此可见，"种植好牡丹，必取洛阳土"，这一民间谚语千真万确，而欧阳修的"洛阳地脉花最宜"，也不是一句虚话、套话。

2 厚重的历史人文环境
Long History and Rich Culture

　　洛阳有着"河山拱戴"之势，"形势甲于天下"，自古洛阳都是历代帝王理想的建都之地。从夏朝都斟鄩开始，商都西亳、西周成王营建洛邑、东周平王迁都洛邑、东汉都雒阳、曹魏都洛阳、西晋都洛阳、北魏迁都洛阳、隋建东都、武周改东都为神都、后梁迁西都洛阳、后唐迁都洛京到后晋建都洛阳，先后有13个王朝在此建都，长达1500多年，洛阳为中国历史上建都时间最早、朝代最多、建都时

Surrounded by mountains and rivers, Luoyang's location is very critical in China. It has been the ideal place for emperors to build their capital since ancient times. There are altogether 13 dynasties establishing the capital in Luoyang and places nearby, including Zhenxun (a place near Luoyang) in the Xia Dynasty, Xibo (a place near Luoyang) in the Shang Dynasty, Luoyi (part of Luoyang) in the West Zhou Dynasty, Luoyi (part of Luoyang) in the East Zhou Dynasty, Luoyang in the East Han Dynasty, Luoyang during Cao Wei period , Luoyang in the West Jin Dynasty, Luoyang in the North Wei period , Luoyang as the east capital of the Sui Dynasty, Luoyang as Shendu during the reign of Empress Wu, Luoyang in the Later Liang Dynasty, Luoyang in the Later Tang Dynasty, and Luoyang in the Later Jin Dynasty. The whole time of Luoyang and places nearby being capital is as long as more than 1500 years, making Luoyang the earliest capital, the longest capital and capital of most dynasties. Sima Guang of the Song Dynasty once wrote, "To know the changes in history, you only need to visit Luoyang."

Heluo district, centered by Luoyang, was called Henan (the south of the Yellow River) in history. It was the earliest political center of Chinese people. Luoyang, or Luo for short, was named based on its location, the former north bank of the Luoshui River. Being between the Luoshui River and the Yellow River, and in the middle of China, it combines the honesty and sincerity of central China, and the beauty and romance of the south together. As the earliest political capital of China and the cradle of Chinese culture and spirit, it is the spiritual capital of China, the earliest China, authentic China and well-established China. Its culture is the epitome of Chinese civilization, the center and symbol of how Chinese culture grows from the beginning to prosperity. Many legends of ancient China originated in Luoyang such as Fu Xi (the first of the Three Sovereigns of ancient China), Nü Wa (the goddess who made human in legends), Huang Di (a legendary Chinese sovereign and culture hero), Yao, Shun and Yu (three of the Three Sovereigns and Five Emperors in Chinese history). According to the record of historical document, "Luoyang is the birth-land of Chinese civilization, Taoism, Confucianism, metaphysics, Buddhism, Confucian classics studies

间最长的城市。因此宋代司马光有诗云："若问古今兴废事，请君只看洛阳城。"

以洛阳城为中心的河洛地区，历史上被称为"河南"，是华夏民族最早的政治活动中心。洛阳，简称"洛"，因地处古洛水北岸而得名，立河洛之间，居天下之中，既禀中原大地敦厚磅礴之气，也具南国水乡妩媚风流之质。她不仅是中国最早的政治首都，更是中华思想与文化的源头圣地，可谓中华民族历史的精神首都，是最早的中国，也是最本色的中国、最渊深的中国，是中华文化的读本和华夏文化从萌芽、成长走向繁荣、壮大的中心和象征。中国古代伏羲、女娲、黄帝、尧、舜、禹等神话传说多传于此。另有史学考证，"文明首萌于此，道学肇始于此，儒学渊源于此，经学兴盛于此，佛学首传于此，玄学形成于此，理学寻源于此"。她是中国5000年文明历史中最为古老的帝都王城，华夏、中华、中土、中国、中原、中州等称谓均源自古老的洛阳城和河洛文明。洛阳二里头遗址距今3800—3500年，相当于中国历史上的夏、商时代。1960年在二里头遗址的上层发现一处规模宏大的宫殿基址，被认为是夏朝都城所在。

and Neo-Confucianism." As Luoyang is the earliest capital in China's five thousand years' history, many Chinese names of China, including Huaxia, Zhonghua, Zhongtu, Zhongguo, Zhongyuan and Zhongzhou originated from ancient Luoyang and Heluo civilization. Luoyang's Erlitou Site dates back to 3500 to 3800 years ago, to the Xia and Shang Dynasties in history. In 1960, archaeologists found a large palace relic site on the top layer of Erlitou Site and they believed that it was the capital of the Xia Dynasty.

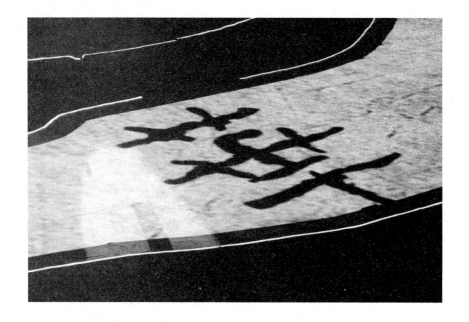

Luoyang is also the headstream of Chinese family names, and root of Minnan people and Hakka people. It has China's earliest historical document *He Tu Luo Shu* *(Paintings from the Yellow River and Book from the Luo River)*. Fu Xi, the father of Chinese culture, based on *He Tu Luo Shu* invented the Eight Diagrams and Jiu Chou (nine laws on how to govern a nation). Later, Shang and Zhou Dynasties built nine tripod cauldrons in Heluo district, symbolizing the unification of China. The Duke of Zhou formulated rules on courtesy. Confucius asked about courtesy. These scholars, politicians, intellectuals, together with many scientists in Luoyang made a great contribution to Chinese civilization and are bright stars in Chinese history. Luoyang is closely related to the origin and development of Chinese traditional cultures: Confucianism, Buddhism and Taoism. It also has close relations with the four great inventions of ancient China. Ban Gu compiled *The History of Han Dynasty*, and Xu Shen wrote *Shuo Wen Jie Zi (Explaining and Analyzing Characters)*. Sima Guang finished *Zi Zhi Tong Jian (Comprehensive Mirror to Aid in Government)*. Cai Lun developed papermaking technology and Yu Chu wrote *Zhou Shuo (Stories of Zhou)*. Chen Shou finished *San Guo Zhi (The History of the Three Kingdoms)* and Ouyang Xiu produced *Xin Tang Shu (New History of the Tang Dynasty)* and *Xin Wu Dai Shi (New History of the Five Dynasties)*. Cheng Yi and Cheng Hao, famous Seven Scholars of Jian'an, Seven Sages of the Bamboo Grove, and twenty-four talents of Jin Valley were gathered in Luoyang, writing wonderful works. All these great events formed Heluo culture and Heluo civilization which are centered by Luoyang and become

洛阳是中华姓氏之根，闽南、客家之根。中华民族最早的历史文献《河图洛书》出自洛阳。被奉为"人文之祖"的伏羲氏，根据河图和洛书画成了八卦和九畴。从此，汤、武定九鼎于河洛，周公"制礼作乐"，孔子入周问礼，洛阳历代科学泰斗、学术流派、鸿生巨儒、翰墨精英，更是照耀史册，灿若繁星。中国传统文化儒、佛、道的产生和发展与洛阳密切相关，中国四大发明与洛阳息息相连。班固修《汉书》，许慎著《说文解字》，司马光编修《资治通鉴》，蔡伦发明造纸术，虞初著《周说》，陈寿编《三国志》，欧阳修编《新唐书》《新五代史》等，无一不得益于洛阳这块沃土。程颐、程颢兄弟，"建安七子""竹林七贤""金谷二十四友"等云集此地，留下享誉九州的名篇。以洛阳为中心的河洛文化和河洛文明，是中华民族文化的核心和源头，构成了华夏文明的重要组成部分。

　　有人说，洛阳是世界上唯一能号称国色天香的古都。5000年文明史，4000余年建城史，1000多年建都史，是我国建都时间最长的古都，兼具自然之美、人文之美、思想之美、城市之美，是人类最早的"山水城市""园林城市"。美国城市规划学家西蒙兹教授称这里是人类"古代最佳人居环境城市"。洛阳，这座承载过十三朝文明的古都，曾经是光耀万丈的世界焦点。现在，洛阳有世界文化遗产1处（龙门石窟），国家重点文物保护单位21处，省级重点文物保护单位77处，馆藏文物近40万件，拥有龙门石窟、白马寺、关林、五大都城遗址、"天子驾六"博物馆等众多文物古迹，并有举世瞩目的小浪底水利枢纽工程，白云山、龙峪湾、花果山国家森林公园和伏

the core, the cradle and an important part of Chinese culture and civilization.

Luoyang is said to be the only ancient capital that has national beauty and celestial fragrance in the world. Its 5000 years' history of civilization, 4000 years' history of city development, and more than 1000 years' history of being capital make it the longest capital in China. Embodying the beauty of nature, culture, thoughts and city, it is the earliest Landscape City and Garden City of human history. Prof. Simmons, an American city planner once said that Luoyang is the most suitable place to live in ancient times. As the capital of thirteen dynasties, it was the focus of the world. Now Luoyang has one World Cultural Heritage site (the Longmen Grottoes), twenty-one important heritage sites under state protection, seventy-seven heritage sites under provincial protection and about four hundred thousand antiques protected in museums. It not only has cultural relics and historic sites like the Longmen Grottoes, White Horse Temple, Guan Lin Temple, relics of five ancient capitals, and Museum of Luoyang Eastern Zhou Royal Horse and Chariot Pits, but also scenic spots like Xiaolangdi project, Baiyun Mountain, Longyu Bay, Huaguo Mountain National Forest Park and Funiu National Nature Reserve. Luoyang has been rated as China's Outstanding Tourist City, China's Top Ten Charming City, China's Noted City and Worth Recommending City of China.

牛山国家级自然保护区等风景名胜，先后荣膺中国优秀旅游城市、中国十大最佳魅力城市、感动世界的中国品牌城市和最值得向世界推介的十大中国名城等称号。

3 牡丹花都里的牡丹文化
Peony Culture in the Capital of Peony

牡丹文化是洛阳城市文化的重要标签之一，它根植于洛阳的历史，受厚重洛阳文化的熏陶，最后结出了"甲天下"的洛阳牡丹。

洛阳牡丹始于隋，盛于唐，而"甲天下"于宋，至今已有1500多年的历史。在这漫长的历史进程中，洛阳牡丹不仅以其雍容华贵、国色天香而美誉遐迩，也以其造化钟情，天下君临而总领群芳。洛阳也成为人们心目中的牡丹之圣地。洛阳牡丹栽培始于隋朝，隋炀帝

Peony culture is one important part of Luoyang culture. It is rooted in Luoyang history, influenced by rich Luoyang culture and harvests the best peony in China.

Peony planting in Luoyang started during the Sui Dynasty, became popular in the Tang Dynasty, and gained nationwide fame in the Song Dynasty. Its history is more than 1500 years. During long time development, Luoyang peony becomes well-known for its beauty, elegance and celestial fragrance. Cultivated by rich culture and suitable environment, it is regarded as the king of flowers. Luoyang therefore becomes the paradise of peony in Chinese people's eyes. According to historical record, the planting of peony started when Emperor Yang of the Sui Dynasty built Xi Yuan (the west garden) with the circumference of 200 *li* (100 kilometers) and introduced twenty boxes of tree peonies of different species from Yizhou. Gao Cheng of the Song Dynasty, who studied the origin of plants and animals also believed that peony planting began during the reign of Emperor Yang.

During the Tang Dynasty, Luoyang, as the vice capital, enlarged its peony planting area and had people specialized in peony planting. There was a man named Song Shanfu in Luoyang who was very good at peony planting. He developed many peony species with different red and white colors. People had no idea of how he made it. At that time, peony flowers had at least five colors: dark red, dark purple, pink, white and yellow. Multi-layer-petal peony also appeared. Besides, Emperor Zhuang of the Later Tang Dynasty once built Lin Fang Palace (Palace of Fragrance) in Luoyang and planted thousands of tree peonies in front of it. The planting area was no smaller than the Tang Palace in Chang'an.

In the North Song Dynasty, the planting area of peony in Luoyang ranked the top in China. Luoyang peony was praised as the best in China and people in Luoyang did not call peony Mudan (peony in Chinese) but Hua (flower in Chinese). They called it Hua because in their eyes, peony was the only flower. Every spring, people of different classes would all plant peony, and even people in poor families did so. When peony flowers blossomed, all citizens, whether scholars or common people, went out and

"周二百里为西苑……易州进二十箱牡丹"，并记述了牡丹品种名称。北宋高承也称"隋炀帝世始传牡丹"。

到了唐朝，作为陪都的洛阳，牡丹的发展更加广泛，并出现了从事牡丹栽培的专业人员。"洛人宋单父，善种牡丹，凡牡丹变异千种，红白斗色，人不能知其术。"当时牡丹至少有5种颜色：殷红、深紫、桃红、通白、黄色，同时出现了重瓣品种。后唐庄宗曾"在洛阳建临芳殿，殿前植牡丹千余本"，其规模不亚于长安唐宫。

北宋时，洛阳牡丹规模为全国之冠。牡丹出"洛阳者，为天下第一也"。洛阳人对牡丹不呼其名，直曰花。"其宰谓天下真花独牡丹"。"春时，城中无贵贱皆插花，虽负担者亦然；花开时，士庶况为遨游。"可见，洛阳人养牡丹、赏牡丹已成为民风民俗。牡丹的栽培技艺也普遍提高，在播种繁殖的同时，用嫁接的方法固定变异，使得新品种不断出现。

当时，最有名的两个品种为"姚黄"和"魏紫"。姚黄出自洛阳司马坡的姚氏家，魏紫出自晋宰相魏仁溥家。洛阳地方留守钱惟演赏之曰："人谓牡丹花王，'姚黄'真可谓王，而'魏紫'乃后也"。北宋时洛阳不仅成为中国牡丹栽培中心，同时出现了一批具有重要学术价值的牡丹专著，为牡丹研究推广及发展做出了杰出的贡献。景祐元年（公元1034年）欧阳修著有《洛阳牡丹记》，列举牡丹名品24种，总结了牡丹栽培、育种经验，记述了洛阳人种花、赏花习俗。这是世界上第一部具有重要学术价值的牡丹专著。其后，周师厚的《洛阳牡丹记》《洛阳花木记》，列举牡丹109种、芍药41种。元祐年间（公元1086—1093年）张峋撰《洛阳花谱》，列牡

appreciated their beauty. It thus can be concluded that planting and appreciating peony had been a tradition in Luoyang. During that period, peony cultivation techniques were greatly improved. While enlarging the scale of planting, people used grafting to develop new species. "No grafting, no good species," many new species were developed by grafting.

At that time, the two most famous peony species were Yao Huang (Yao's Yellow) and Wei Zi (Wei's purple). Yao Huang was bred by Yao family living in Sima Terrace, Luoyang and Wei Zi was developed by Wei Renpu's family, a chef minister of the Jin Dynasty. Qian Weiyan, the official of Luoyang once exclaimed, "People always say that peony is the king of flowers, but I have to say Yao Huang indeed can be the king and Wei Zi be the queen." During the Song Dynasty, Luoyang being the center of peony planting, witnessed the appearance of several important works on peony which made a great contribution to the promotion of peony studies and its development. Ouyang Xiu wrote *Luoyang Peony* in the first year of the reign of Jingyou (1034), listing 24 peony species, summarizing experience of peony planting and breeding, and recording the custom of Luoyang people in peony planting and appreciating. It is the first academic works specializing in peony in the world. Zhou Shihou wrote *Luoyang Peony* and *Luoyang Flowers*, listing 109 peony species and 41 Chinese peony species in 1082. Zhang Xun finished *Illustrated Book on Peony of Luoyang* during 1086 to 1093, depicting 119 species. These books not only encouraged peony planting but also provided valuable information for current peony studies.

Luoyang has a rich peony culture, which is an important part of Heluo culture and a distinct component of Chinese civilization. Since the Tang and Song dynasties, many poems, lyrics, novels, stories, paintings and embroideries have been made to express people's love for peony. Because of people's attachment to peony, legends and stories related to peony become well spread and are passed down generation after generation. In those stories and legends, peony is described as a beautiful and kind fairy who helps poor people and never yields to power, embodying people's wish and ideal. After People's Republic of China was founded in 1949, archaeologists found many valuable antiques about peony in ancient tombs. These antiques, together with existing peony images on ancient architecture,

丹119种。这些专著对促进当时牡丹栽培发展及后人研究牡丹提供了珍贵的资料。

洛阳具有丰富的牡丹文化，它是河洛文化的重要组成部分，是华夏民族文化的一朵奇葩。从唐宋开始出现的赞颂牡丹的诗词、歌赋、小说、故事以及绘画、刺绣等量大且内容丰富。由于人们对洛阳牡丹的至爱，千百年来流传的关于洛阳牡丹的种种神话故事和趣闻逸事更是家喻户晓。人们把牡丹比作造福人类的天使、反抗强权的正义化身，把它塑造成美丽、善良的仙女等，寄托了人们的理想和愿望。新中国成立后，洛阳考古发掘墓葬中发现的有关表现牡丹内容的珍贵文物以及现存的古代建筑上的牡丹纹饰，是研究牡丹史、绘画史、建筑史、雕刻艺术史等不可多得的资料。表现牡丹题材的戏剧歌曲、影视音乐以及工艺美术等作品争奇斗妍，琳琅满目。

纵观洛阳牡丹的发展史就是一部中国历代兴亡的演变史，李格非叹曰："且天下之治乱，候于洛阳之盛衰而知；洛阳之盛衰，候于园圃之废兴而得"。但无论历史如何兴衰，洛阳的牡丹始终最娇艳。洛阳牡丹文化的发展，不仅推动了整个河洛地域牡丹文化的发展，也为形成中国的牡丹文化奠定了基础。洛阳与牡丹之间的不解之缘，令洛阳牡丹花都之名当之无愧。

are very important for the study of peony history, painting history, architecture history and carving history. There are also many peony-related dramas, songs, and handicraft works, enriching people's life.

The history of peony mirrors the history of China. Li Gefei, a writer of the Song Dynasty said, "The development of China can be seen from the development of Luoyang. And the development of Luoyang can be seen from the development of its peony gardens." No matter how time changes, Luoyang always has the brightest peony flowers. The development of peony culture in Luoyang not only promotes the development of peony culture in Heluo district, but also lays a solid foundation for Chinese peony culture. Luoyang's indissoluble bond with peony makes Luoyang merit its title: The Capital of Peony.

第三章

洛阳牡丹节

　　中国洛阳牡丹文化节的前身是洛阳牡丹花会，是由当地传统的赏花习俗发展而来的民俗节日。洛阳牡丹甲天下，赏牡丹花是洛阳人民的传统习俗。每年洛阳牡丹花开的季节，全城人民都会进行盛大的赏花活动。而到现代社会，每年的赏花盛会就更加隆重和热闹，当地居民，中外游客，齐集于此，观赏争妍斗艳的牡丹鲜花，感受悠久深厚的牡丹文化，体验传统热闹的民俗活动。

Chapter Three

Luoyang Peony Festival

The predecessor of Luoyang Peony Cultural Festival of China is Luoyang Peony Festival, a folk festival that develops from local custom of peony appreciating. Luoyang peony is the best in China and it is a tradition of Luoyang people to appreciate peony flowers. Every year when the flowers blossom, they hold large events for peony appreciating. As time goes by, the peony festival becomes larger and more popular. Luoyang people, and visitors from home and abroad get together in Luoyang, appreciate beautiful peony flowers, experience rich peony culture and participate in interesting folk activities.

1

从习俗到节日：洛阳牡丹节的起源与发展
From Custom to Festival: the Origin and Development of Luoyang Peony Festival

The origin and development of Luoyang peony festival can be seen from two perspectives: folk activities and government's organization.

1.The folk origin: custom of peony appreciating in history

Seen from the folk perspective, the origin of Luoyang peony festival dates back to long time ago. It is closely related to peony planting and the development of peony culture, and can at least date back to 1400 years ago, during the reign of Emperor Yang. Since Emperor Yang of the Sui Dynasty introduced peony to Luoyang for ornamentation, peony appreciating activities had started. According to historical records, when peony flowers blossomed, Emperor Yang would go to

追溯洛阳牡丹节的起源与发展，应该从民间与官方两个层面分别进行。

一、民间发源：历史上的赏花习俗

从民间追溯来看，洛阳牡丹节的起源与发展历史非常悠久，它与洛阳牡丹花的栽培种植以及洛阳牡丹文化的形成和发展息息相关，其源头至少可追溯到1400多年前的隋炀帝时期。隋朝将牡丹花作为观赏植物引入洛阳，开启了洛阳牡丹赏花活动的源头。史载，每当牡丹花开的时候，隋炀帝常常带着嫔妃宫女和文武百官在皇宫西苑牡丹园里赏花游玩，饮酒作乐，并配以歌舞表演，有时还通宵达旦地娱乐。有皇帝做榜样，朝臣民子争相效仿，赏花开始成为大众习俗。每年春季，洛阳城内，人们三五成群，竞相赏花。可见，从隋朝起，洛阳牡丹赏花活动就被作为一种国事活动而备受推崇。

至唐宋时期，赏牡丹已成为全城人民春季的重要活动，欧阳修在《洛阳牡丹记·风俗记》对此中作了较为详尽的叙述："洛阳之俗，大抵好花，春时，城中无贵贱皆插花，虽负担者亦然。花开时，士庶竞为遨游。往往于古寺废宅有池台处为市井，张幄幕，笙歌之声相闻。"鄞江周氏著《洛阳牡丹记》中也有记载："姚黄……故洛人贵之，号为花王。城中每岁不过开三数朵，都人士女，必倾城往观，乡人扶老携幼，不远千里，其为时所贵重如此。"邵雍在《洛阳春吟》中写道："洛阳

the peony garden with his concubines, maids and ministers to admire flowers, drink wines and enjoy songs and dances there. Sometimes they even stayed there overnight. Influenced by the emperor, officials and common people also liked to appreciate peony flowers, which gradually became a folk custom. Every spring, they would go in group to admire beautiful peony flowers. This shows that since the Sui Dynasty, peony appreciating in Luoyang had been a popular national event.

During the Tang and Song Dynasties, peony appreciating was an important activity for Luoyang people in spring. Ouyang Xiu once described it in detail in *Luoyang Peony: the Customs*, "It's a tradition of Luoyang people to appreciate peony. In spring, all people, poor or rich, pick peony flowers and put them in vases or pots, even the poorest do so. When peony flowers bloom, they all go outside and admire the flowers' beauty. Setting up tents in old temples and deserted houses with pavilions and platforms, they sing songs and play music instruments, having a good time." Zhou Shihou from Yinjiang also depicted it in his *Luoyang Peony*, "Yao Huang is praised by Luoyang people as the king of flowers. Every year the total number of its flowers is no more than thirty. But people in Luoyang, old and young, rich and poor, male and female, all travel many miles to have a look. They indeed really like it." Shao Yong in *Luoyang Spring* wrote that, "Luoyang people have seen so many gorgeous flowers or they do not regard peach flower or plum flower as flowers. They can not feel endlessly happy until peony flowers bloom." In the Song Dynasty, Luoyang was designated as the west capital and people had a relatively well-off life. They were so fond of peony that they did not call peony Mudan (peony in Chinese), but Hua(flower in Chinese). For them, peony is the only flower in China. Later, no matter how dynasties change, the custom of peony appreciating remains.

Before 1983 when the First Luoyang Peony Festival was held, peony appreciating was only a custom and did not have a specific name. Only *Mo Zhuang Man Lu (Writings in Mo Village)* recorded that Qian Wei, an official of Luoyang in the Song Dynasty once held Ten Thousand Flowers Festival, "As Luoyang peony became well-known in China, Qian once held Ten-thousand Flowers Festival when peony flowers blossomed. He used flowers as screens and bamboo tubes with flowers as beams and arches to place peony flowers everywhere." But the book did not mention whether this was held in Qian's house privately or in a public place for all people in Luoyang to participate. Due to historical reasons, the festival did not last long. Though peony appreciating in Luoyang did not have an official name, it met all the requirements for a festival: specific time and place, a certain number of people

人惯见奇葩，桃李花开未当花。须是牡丹花盛发，满城方始乐无涯。"北宋时，洛阳作为西京，人们生活较为富裕，当时的洛阳人喜爱牡丹已到了情有独钟的地步，对牡丹不称呼其名，"直曰花，其意谓天下真花独牡丹"。随后，无论朝代如何变更，洛阳赏花习俗始终延续了下来。

然而，在1983年举办第一届洛阳牡丹花会之前，洛阳牡丹赏花活动几乎一直都只是以一项传统习俗存在于历史，并未有一个确切的节日名称，仅《墨庄漫录》中有记载宋代西京太守钱惟曾举办过万花会："西京牡丹闻于天下，花盛时，太守作万花会，宴集之所，以花为屏帐，至于梁栋柱拱，悉心竹筒贮水，簪花钉挂，举目皆花也。"但文献中也未记载这万花会到底只是办于太守府中，还是全城人民齐参与的活动，且由于历史原因，该节庆最终未能延续下来。尽管如此，洛阳赏花习俗虽一直未有节日之名，但却早就有节日之实。根据节日要有"固定的时间、固定的地方、固定的参与人群与固定的仪式或活动内容"来看，洛阳牡丹赏花活动早已具备成为一个节日的基本条件，因此，现代社会下洛阳牡丹文化节的举办可以说是历史的必然。

二、政府的组织与推动

从官方记载来看，洛阳牡丹节的起源和发展历史并不长，从1983年第一届洛阳牡丹花会举办至今，共30余年时间。1982年，洛阳市人大常委会通过决议，命名牡丹花为洛阳市"市花"，并决定根据牡丹花期的情况于每年4月至5月举办洛阳牡丹花会。1983年4月15—25日，洛阳市举办了第一届洛阳牡丹花会，共接待来自7个国家、地区和全

participating, and distinct customs and activities. The holding of Luoyang peony festival in modern times thus is inevitable.

2.Government's organization and promotion

Seen from the government's perspective, Luoyang Peony Festival does not have a long history. The first Luoyang Peony Festival was held in 1983 and it had been held 30 times by 2012. In 1982, the Standing Committee of Luoyang People's Congress passed the resolution to designate peony as the city flower

and hold Luoyang Peony Festival every April to May based on peony's flowering phase. During April 15 to 25, 1983, Luoyang held its first peony festival, receiving 2.5 million visitors (person-time) from 22 provinces of China and 7 other countries and regions. In 1991, Henan Provincial Party Committee and Henan Provincial Government decided to change the name of Luoyang Peony Festival to Luoyang Peony Festival of Henan and promote it as a provincial festival. In 2008, Luoyang Peony Festival got into the list of National Intangible Cultural Heritage and became one of the four famous festivals in China[1]. In November 2010, it was approved by the Ministry of Culture to become a national festival and was named as Luoyang Peony Cultural Festival of China, cohosted by the Ministry of Culture and government of Henan Province. In 2012, to further promote the festival and enlarge its influence, the organizer of Luoyang Peony Cultural Festival of China designed its emblem, mascots and slogan, integrating the elements of Luoyang, peony and culture altogether. The emblem is an important symbol of peony festival. The Chinese character "洛" (Luo) is seen as the main body to depict blooming peony flowers, flying dragon and waves of the Yellow River. Another Chinese character "文" is integrated into "洛", combining Luoyang and culture together. The mascots are image representatives of Luoyang Peony Festival. Based on the cartoon image of Luoyang red peony, two lovely girls wearing green leaves as clothes and gold pistils as crown are created, which shows the status of Luoyang peony as the king of flowers. The two girls

[1]The others three festivals are Dalian Fashion Festival, Harbin Ice and Snow Festival and Weifang Kite Festival.

国22个省、市、自治区的游客250万人次。1991年，河南省委、省政府决定将洛阳牡丹花会更名为河南省洛阳牡丹花会，洛阳牡丹花会升格为省级节庆活动。2008年，洛阳牡丹花会入选国家级非物质文化遗产名录，并成为中国四大名会[1]之一。2010年11月，经文化部正式批准，洛阳牡丹花会升格为国家级节会，更名为"中国洛阳牡丹文化节"，由文化部和河南省人民政府主办。2012年，为进行节日品牌的宣传，进一步扩大牡丹文化节的对外影响，"中国洛阳牡丹文化节"确定了集洛阳、牡丹、文化等元素于一身的节徽、吉祥物和主题宣传口号。其中，节徽是牡丹文化节的重要标志，标志以汉字"洛"融合"文"变形为主体设计核心，勾勒出绽放的牡丹、腾飞的祥龙、黄河浪潮等元素，"洛阳"融合"文化"。

[1]洛阳牡丹花会与大连服装节、哈尔滨冰灯节、潍坊风筝节并称中国四大名会。

吉祥物是牡丹文化节的形象代表，以"洛阳红"牡丹卡通形象为元素，以花为头、绿叶为衣，花蕊为冠，表示洛阳拥有"花之冠、花中王"的"国花"美誉。取名"红红"和"丹丹"，则寓意洛阳红牡丹，也寓意洛阳人民构建"中国牡丹城、和谐新洛阳"的一片"丹"心。主题宣传口号是牡丹文化节的重要对外宣传语，为"千年帝都神韵，满城国色天香"。

从1983年举办至今，中国洛阳牡丹文化节已成功举办30届，逐步成为全国起步较早、规模较大、坚持较好的节会品牌。经过30年的积极探索，洛阳牡丹节经历了一个逐步发展壮大的过程。

一是规模由小到大。1983年，第一届洛阳牡丹花会举办之时，全市仅有王城公园等少数牡丹观赏点。如今，洛阳市已建立了国内规模最大的牡丹基因库，品种千余，规模观

are named Honghong (red) and Dandan (sincerity), representing Luoyang red peony and Luoyang people's sincerity of building the city of peony in China and a new harmonious Luoyang. The slogan "Charm of a thousand-year-old city, national beauty and celestial fragrance of peony all over Luoyang" also plays an important role in the festival promotion.

红红　丹丹
Honghong　Dandan

Since 1983, Luoyang has successfully held 30 Luoyang peony festivals and gradually created a brand that was established early, continues successfully and has large participation. During thirty years' active exploration, Luoyang peony festival grows quickly.

First, from small to large. When the First Luoyang Peony Festival was held in 1983, there were only Wangcheng Park and a few other places for peony appreciating and only two million visitors (person-time) went to the festival per year. Now, Luoyang has the largest peony gene bank in China with more than one thousand species, eleven large gardens and parks for peony appreciating, and nearly thirty thousand *mu*'s (about two thousand hectares) planting area. Its peonies are sold to more than twenty countries and regions in southeast Asia, Europe and America. The total number of viewing sites in Luoyang now is more than ninety, including Wangcheng Park, Peony Garden, National Peony Garden, Shenzhou Peony Garden, National Flower Garden, Baiyun Mountain, Jiguandong Gaoshan Peony Garden,etc.. This enables a three-stage peony bloom from downtown, outskirt, to the south mountainous area. Besides, thanks to the technique development on peony's flowering period, visitors are able to appreciate peony flowers during the whole festival. The festival now has developed from a peony appreciating activity to a comprehensive event that combines peony appreciating, lantern show, tourism, trade, cultural activities, and sports together.

Second, from city level to national level. Luoyang peony festival at first was held by Luoyang government and its aim was to make more friends while appreciating flowers. In 1991, Henan Provincial Party Committee and Henan Provincial Government decided to make peony festival a provincial event and change its name to Luoyang Peony Festival of Henan, creating a new model that uses Luoyang as the platform to exhibit the whole province's achievements. Peony festival, therefore, became an important media for Henan Province to incentivize investments attract intellectuals, draw exhibitions and conferences, and boost its tourism. In 2010, approved by the Ministry of Culture, Luoyang

赏园区11个，种植面积近3万亩，商品牡丹远销东南亚、欧美等20多个国家和地区；新建、改建王城公园、牡丹公园、国家牡丹园、神州牡丹园、国花园以及白云山、鸡冠洞高山牡丹园等牡丹观赏点90余处，实现了市区、市郊和南部山区的牡丹梯次开放，再加上牡丹花期控制技术的基本成熟，使游客在整个花会期间都能够欣赏到牡丹，牡丹节也从单纯的牡丹观赏发展成为集赏花观灯、旅游观光、经济贸易、文化体育于一体的大型综合性节会活动。

二是规格由低到高。洛阳牡丹文化节举办之初仅仅是由洛阳市主办，办节宗旨也仅仅是以花为媒，广交朋友。1991年，河南省委、省政府把牡丹花会确定为全省性重大节会，并更名为"河南省洛阳牡丹花会"，进一步形成了洛阳搭台、全省唱戏的崭新模式，使牡丹花会发展成为河南省招商引资、招才引智、招展引会、招团引游的重要平台。2010

年，经文化部批准，河南省洛阳牡丹花会升格为国家级节庆活动，更名为"中国洛阳牡丹文化节"。

三是影响由近及远。牡丹文化节举办之初，游客主要是洛阳市及周边地区群众，客商主要是河南省及国内企业。如今，赏花观光游客来自世界各地，参加经贸洽谈的客商遍及世界各地，外商及国外游客由最初的1000多人发展为数万人。

四是会期由短到长。牡丹文化节最初确定为每年的4月15—25日，为期10天。为进一步扩大牡丹花会的规模、影响和拉动作用，并适应气候、花期等自然条件的变化，2005年将会期改为每年的4月1日至5月5日，使花会延长为一个月，形成了牡丹花会与"五一"黄金周相连的"旅游黄金月"现象。

五是效益由少到多。举办牡丹文化节之初，活动项目较少，经贸活动成

Peony Festival of Henan was named as Luoyang Peony Cultural Festival of China, becoming a national event.

Third, from Luoyang to abroad. When the first Luoyang peony festival was held, most visitors were from Luoyang and places nearby. Enterprises doing business there were mainly local ones or Chinese enterprises. Now visitors and enterprises conducting business in the festival are from all over the world and the number of foreign businessmen and visitors increases from more than one thousand in the beginning to dozens of thousand.

Fourth, from ten days to more than one month. At first the peony festival was held during April 15th to April 25th every year. Later, to further enlarge the scope and influence of peony festival and adapt to the change of natural conditions like climate and flowering period, the duration of the festival was lengthened to more than one month, from April 1st to May 5th in 2005, covering the May Day holidays.

Fifth, from low profits to high profits. There were only a few activities in the beginning and the volume of business conducted there was only several or dozens of million *yuan*. Now, the peony festival is a gold season to attract investments. With many commercial activities, the volume of business conducted during the festival is more than a hundred billion *yuan*.

Sixth, from large input to small input. In the past, the total cost of peony festival was borne by local government and local enterprises. In recent years, through marketization of the festival, government only needs to provide capital for the promotion and related governmental activities. Other money is gained from the market.

交额仅有数百万、数千万元；如今，每年牡丹文化节都成为招商引资的黄金季节，经贸活动硕果累累，总成交额已高达千亿元。

六是投入由多到少。过去，牡丹花会经费全靠政府投入，或通过行政手段向企业集资摊派，近几年花会活动主要采取市场化运作，政府仅仅投入宣传经费和政务活动经费，举办资金主要通过市场化运作筹集。

2 交织在传统与现代之间：丰富多彩的节日活动

Various Festival Activities: Combining Tradition with Modern Elements

从民间传统赏花习俗到洛阳牡丹花会再到中国洛阳牡丹文化节，节日的规模越来越大，展示了一个地方民俗节日从形成到发展再走向繁荣的过程。在全球化进程的影响下，洛阳牡丹文化节也将会朝着具有国际型综合影响力的节日继续发展。

由于洛阳牡丹文化节是从民间赏花习俗演变而来，节日并没有固定的仪式与过程，具有一定的随意性，因此，在洛阳牡丹文化节中，大家可根据大会主办方所准备的日程安

From a folk custom to Luoyang Peony Festival, then to Luoyang Peony Cultural Festival of China, the activity of peony appreciating in Luoyang gains greater and greater influence and scope, showing the process of a local festival developing from none to prosperity. Under the influence of globalization, Luoyang Peony Cultural Festival will further become a festival with international influence.

As Luoyang peony festival develops from a folk custom, it does not have fixed procedure or ceremony and can be arranged according to specific circumstances. During the festival, visitors can choose activities they like and make their own arrangement according to the official schedule. Take the official schedule of the 30th Luoyang

Peony Cultural Festival as an example: though the festival lasted one month, some activities such as peony appreciating had one month duration, while others like exhibitions and performance only lasted one or a few days. Based on the official schedule and personal interests, visitors can enjoy their own Luoyang Peony Cultural Festival.

Compared with other festivals, Luoyang Cultural Peony Festival is longer and covers larger areas. Its festival activities are also more diverse, including not only traditional flower appreciating, folk fair, poetry reading and lantern show, but also modern comic con, auto show, and concerts. Economic cooperation, trade fair, and symposiums are also held during the festival to promote regional development and boost the exchanges and development of science and culture.

排进行活动选择，也可以自主安排自己的过节日程。以2012年第30届"中国洛阳牡丹文化节"为例，节日历时一个月，有些活动如"牡丹赏花系列活动"一直贯穿整个节日，有些活动如展览、文艺展演等活动只是一天到几天的时间，活动与活动之间的时间安排既有区别又有重叠，整个牡丹文化节的日程安排非常紧凑。前来过节的游客们可根据每年节日的日程安排与自己的兴趣爱好来计划属于自己的"洛阳牡丹文化节"。

洛阳牡丹文化节节庆时间较长，节日地域范围较大。与一般的节日相比较，洛阳牡丹文化节的节日活动更加丰富与多元，不仅有传统的赏花、庙会、诗会、灯会等活动，也有具有现代气息的动漫比赛、车展、明星演唱会等，还有以促进地区发展为目的的经济合作、贸易投资洽谈会，促进科学文化事业发展与交流的学术研讨会等各种类型的活动。

一、传统型活动

（一）牡丹花会

牡丹花会，即赏花活动，可以说是洛阳牡丹文化节的传统性和代表性节目，是整个节日活动的主体之一。每年四月间，洛阳城中牡丹花开遍，雍容华贵淡淡幽香，满城花海，游人如织，赶花市赏花展。洛阳作为中国最大的牡丹观赏胜地之一，每年牡丹花会期间接待游客百万人次以上。其时各个品种的牡丹花争相绽放，争奇斗艳：最绿的牡丹是近于叶绿的"豆绿"；最黑的牡丹是"冠世墨玉"；花瓣最多的牡丹是"魏紫"，有六七百片；最红的牡丹是"火炼金丹"；最白的牡丹是"夜光白"；最蓝的牡丹是"蓝田玉"；最佳的间色牡丹是"二乔"；最能以假乱真的"牡丹"是"荷包牡丹"，叶似牡丹而非牡丹。人们在牡丹花海里惊叹陶醉，流连忘返。目前，洛阳全市共有成规模

1. Traditional activities

Peony fair

Peony fair, i.e. peony appreciating, is the most traditional and representative activity, and one of the major events of Luoyang Peony Cultural Festival. Every April, peony flowers bloom all over Luoyang. Their elegance and fragrance attract several million visitors to go to Luoyang. As one of China's largest peony viewing resorts, Luoyang receives more than one million tourists (person-time) every year. During the festival, peony flowers of various species all bloom, competing against each other with their beauty and fragrance. The greenest one is Dou Lü (pea's green), almost as green as the leaf and the blackest is Guan Shi Mo Yu (black jade crowning the world). Peony flower with most petals is Wei Zi (Wei's purple), with about six to seven hundred petals. The reddest is Huo Lian Jin Dan (golden pellets in fire) and the whitest is Ye Guang Bai (moonlight's white). The bluest is called Lantian Yu (blue jade of Lantian) and the best dual-color peony flower is named Er Qiao (two famous beautiful ladies of the Three Kingdom Period). There is also one "peony species" He Bao Mudan (pocket peony) which has similar leaves of peony but is not peony. In the sea of flowers, visitors usually marvel at flowers' beauty and forget to leave. Now Luoyang has more than 20 gardens for peony appreciating and its peony planting covers an area of about 16,000 *mu* (more than 1000 hectares). The peony species totals more than 1100, with nine different colors such as black, red, yellow, green, white and purple and the total number of tree peonies is more than 40 million, with more than 10 million tree peonies for appreciating covering an area of 4000 *mu* (about 267 hectares).

As peony appreciating is a traditional custom in Luoyang with more than one thousand years' history, people there have developed their own taste during the long-time peony appreciating.

First, the color of flowers is very important in peony appreciating. That peony is titled as the national flower is closely related to its diverse colors. Its flowers mainly have nine colors: white, red, yellow, pink, purple, black (dark purple), blue, green and multi-colors. Every peony species shows different colors and every color has different variations. Not only the same peony species has different colors in different years, cultivation conditions, light or locations, but also the same flower's color changes in the beginning, the middle and the end of bloom. The most spectacular peony species are Er Qiao and Dao Jin (colorful island). They can have two different colors in the same tree, in the same flower, or even in the same petal. Zi Ban (purple speckle) peony is also worth mentioning: its flowers have

的牡丹观赏园20余个，牡丹种植面积1.6万亩，黑、红、黄、绿、白、紫等9大色系的牡丹品种达1100多个，数量达4000多万株，其中可供观赏的牡丹有4000多亩，1000多万株。

牡丹花会是洛阳地区人们沿袭了千百年的传统习俗，对于牡丹花的欣赏，人们有着自己独特的心得。

首先，要观花色。牡丹能称为"国色"，跟其五彩缤纷的花色是分不开的。牡丹有白色、红色、黄色、粉色、紫色、黑色（墨紫色）、蓝色、绿色和复色等九大色系。不同的牡丹品种，呈现不同的颜色。而每一种颜色，又有深浅浓淡的变化。同一牡丹品种，在不同年份、不同栽培条件和不同光照、不同地点也会有不同的变化。同一朵花在初开、盛开、快要凋谢时花色也会变化。最奇特的是"二乔"和"岛锦"，同一株上甚至同一花朵、同一花瓣上，可同时呈现两种颜色。紫斑牡丹花瓣基部具有明显的色斑，分为红色、棕红色、紫红色和黑色等种。

红色：红牡丹是最常见的牡丹花色，色泽娇艳，引人注目，且红色为中国的喜庆之色，红牡丹更能为喜庆之事添上一分锦色。如"状元红"的由来：相传宋代洛阳一书生家中种了许多牡丹，他终日徜徉于牡丹丛中读书，后来中了状元。当喜报到家时，正值园中牡丹盛开，红艳满眼，书生喜极，大叫"状元红"。红色牡丹比较名贵的品种有国红、红宝石、状元红、朱砂红、火炼金丹、王红、霓虹焕彩、满园春光、百花争春、火炼碧绿等。

黄色：黄牡丹雍容华贵，其中以姚黄最为珍贵。姚黄相传是由宋代洛阳邙山脚下司马坡姚

obvious stains at the base of petals, which can be red, brownish red, purple or black.

Red: red is the most common color of peony flowers. Bright and beautiful red is the happy festive color in China. Therefore, red peony flowers can add more beauty and happiness in festivals and weddings. Take the No. 1 Red peony for example. It is said that there was a scholar in Luoyang who planted a lot of red peony flowers at home and spent most of his time reading among flowers every day. Later he ranked the first in the national examination. When the news arrived, it happened that his peony flowers were in full bloom, forming a red sea. The scholar was very delighted and shouted, "No.1 Red". Other famous red peony species include: Guo Hong (national red), Hong Bao Shi (ruby), Zhu Sha Hong (cinnabar red), Huo Lian Jin Dan (golden pellet in fire), Wang Hong (Wang's red), Ni Hong Huan Cai (Neon's red), Man Yuan Chun Guang (spring in the garden), Bai Hua Zheng Chun (flowers of spring), Huo Lian Bi Lü (green jade in fire), etc..

Yellow: yellow peony flowers are dignified and graceful. Among all yellow peony species, Yao Huang (Yao's yellow) is the most precious. It is believed to be developed by Yao Chong's family of the Song Dynasty on Sima Terrace at the foot of Mangshang Mountain, Luoyang. The flower at first is light yellow but it becomes golden yellow when in full blossom. Being above peony leaves, the flower's petals, as if waxed, look shining and deliver gentle fragrance. Therefore, Yao Huang is called the king of peony. Other rare yellow peony species are: Yu Yi Huang (imperial yellow), Jin Yu Jiao Hui (gold and jade), Chu'e Huang (goslings' yellow), Jin Si Guan Ding (gold silk crown), Zhong Sheng Huang (Zhong's yellow), Gu Tong Yan (bronze face) and Huang He Ling (yellow crane's plume).

Purple: purple peony flowers look vigorous and gorgeous. Of all purple species, the most valuable one is Wei Zi (Wei's purple). It was bred by Wei Renpu's family of the Five Dynasties in Luoyang and its flowers are purplish red, looking like lotus or crown in shape. Because of its long flowering period and plenty of plump flowers, Wei Zi is called the queen of peony. As a traditional important peony species, it has many varieties like Big Wei Zi and Small Wei Zi. Other precious purple species are Zi Xiu Qiu (purple silk ball), Ge Jin Zi (hemp purple), Duo Ye Zi (multi-leaf purple), Zi Chong Lou (purple multi-story building), Da Zong Zi (big bronze purple), Zhu Ye Zi (bamboo leaf's purple), San Ying Shi (three heroes), and Da Ye Zi (large-leaf purple).

Green: green peony flowers are delightful and there are only a few species. Major green peony species include: Ou Bi (Ou's green), Dou Lü (pea's green), Lü Xiang Qiu (green fragrant ball) and Cui Mu (green screen). Among them, Dou Lü (pea's green) is the most rare and precious. Just as the name suggests, its flowers are as green as peas when in

皇家所培育的千叶黄花，花初开为鹅黄色，盛开时金黄色，花开高于叶面，瓣如着蜡，光彩照人，气味清香，有"牡丹花王"之称。其他比较名贵的黄色牡丹品种有御衣黄、金玉交辉、雏鹅黄、金丝冠顶、种生黄、古铜颜、黄鹤翎等。

紫色：紫牡丹热情大气，其中以魏紫系列最为名贵。魏紫出自五代洛阳魏仁溥家。花紫红色，荷花形或皇冠形。花期长，花量大，花朵丰满，被称为"牡丹花后"。魏紫是传统牡丹极品之一，有大魏紫和小魏紫等多个品种。其他较为名贵的还有紫绣球、葛巾紫、多叶紫、紫重楼、大棕紫、竹叶紫、三英士、大叶紫等。

绿色：绿牡丹清新脱俗，但品种不多，主要品种有欧碧、豆绿、绿香球、翠幕等。"豆绿"是牡丹花中的稀有名贵品种，顾名思义，其花开时颜色呈青豆般的绿色，花型呈绣球型，有时也呈皇冠型，内瓣长得很密集，皱皱褶褶地交错在一起。初开时是青绿色，盛开后颜色逐渐变淡。"豆绿"花开娇嫩妩媚，清爽宜人，民间曾流传有"豆绿值千金"的说法。欧碧也是传统牡丹珍品之一，陆游曾考证此花："其花浅碧而开最晚。独出欧氏，故以姓著。"据传，此花初种阳平观。有欧氏女，貌美，善诗文，家遭不幸，入阳平观修行。花开时节，浮游浪子借看花入观滋扰。观主不堪其烦。时有文士暗与欧氏诗文结缘，辗转让欧氏还俗，结为佳偶。观主以此花赠欧氏。后传民间，世人称为欧碧。

蓝色：蓝牡丹别具风情，比较名贵的有蓝田玉、紫蓝魁，另有垂头蓝、迟蓝、水晶蓝、蓝芙蓉、青翠蓝、冷光盘、蓝翠楼等。

blossom. With inner petals growing closely to each other and interlacing together, the flowers look like balls or crowns. When the flower begins to bloom, its color is dark green, and as the flower becomes bigger and bigger, the color becomes lighter and lighter. Because of the delicate and charming flowers, there was a saying that, "One tree of Dou Lü is worthy of one thousand pieces of gold". Ou Bi (Ou's green) is also one of the traditional peony species. Lu You once wrote, "Ou Bi's flower is light green and blooms late. Only Ou's family has this special species, therefore it was named Ou Bi (Ou's green)." It is said that it was at first planted in Yangping Temple where lived a beautiful young lady named Ou who was good at poetry and writing. After her family suffered a misfortune, she went to Yangping Temple and became a nun. But when the peony flowers bloomed, many playboys would go there to harass her under the excuse of peony appreciating, making the host of temple very unhappy. At that time, Ou fell in love with a young scholar during the poem sharing. They got married and the host of temple presented the peony as a gift to them. Later, it was introduced to many places and people named it Ou Bi.

Blue: blue peony is very special and the valuable species include: Lantian Yu (blue jade of Lantian), Zi Lan Kui (purplish blue peony), Chui Tou Lan (head lowering blue), Chi Lan (Chi's blue), Shui Jing Lan (crystal blue), Lan Fu Rong (blue hibiscus), Qing Cui Lan (green blue), Leng Guang Pan (cold-light plate), Lan Cui Lou (blue multi-story house), etc..

White: white peony flowers are pure, unstained and elegant. The most precious ones are Gui Fei Shang Yue (imperial concubine admiring moon) and Ye Guang Bai (moonlight's white). Others include Yu Lou Dian Cui (white jade on green), Xiang Ying Xiao Yue (fragrant moon), Shui Jing Bai (crystal white), Yu Ban Bai (jade's white), Xiang Yu Bai Yu Bing (fragrant jade ice), Xue Qiu (snow ball), and Wu Da Zhou (five continents). Jing Yu (sunlight jade) is a new species developed in the 1970s. When the flower blossoms, it delivers tender fragrance and is large and round like a crown. Its petals look almost transparent, like lotus with droplets. They are also edible and taste a little sweet.

Black: elegant black peony is one of the most precious peony species. Its most famous two species are Hei Hua Kui (black king of flowers) and Hei San Jin (gold on black). According to peony experts, Hei Hua Kui (black king of peony) is quite rarely seen. Technicians of Luoyang National Flower Garden explained that its flower actually is purplish red. As its color is so dark, people regard the peony as black peony. In fact, there is no black peony. Those black peony people called are usually dark red or purplish red. Experts of Wangcheng Park said that though peony has many colors, black peony is quite rare, because the tissues of black flower, especially petals, are very tender and might be hurt easily by high temperature. As black can absorb all light waves, the temperature of black flower grows

白色：白牡丹纤尘不染，纯洁高雅，其中以贵妃赏月、夜光白最为名贵。另外还有玉楼点翠、香迎晓月、水晶白、玉板白、香玉白玉冰、雪球、五大洲等。"景玉"是20世纪70年代新培育的白牡丹品种，花开时，花型呈皇冠样，花大色正，形状丰满。其中花瓣轻薄，透明感强，远远观之，晶莹剔透宛如出水芙蓉，极具观赏性。花朵盛开时，会飘出清香味道，花瓣入口微甜，是食用牡丹品种之一。

黑色：黑牡丹典雅古朴，是牡丹花里弥足珍贵的品种，以黑花魁、黑撒金最为名贵。牡丹专家说，黑花魁是难得的牡丹品种。洛阳国花园的技术员解释黑花魁因"红得发紫"，花大色重，所以有人便视其为黑牡丹。事实上，牡丹家族中没有纯粹的黑牡丹，人们习惯上把深红色、深紫色牡丹称为黑牡丹。王城公园技师介绍说，牡丹花的颜色虽然很多，但黑花十分稀少。这是因为黑花的组织尤其是花瓣一般都比较柔嫩，容易受到高温伤害；黑色可以吸收全部光波，花在阳光下升温快，组织容易受到灼伤，不利于花的自我保护，因此，黑花能自然保存下来的品种寥寥无几。此外，黑色系牡丹之所以珍贵是因为培育不易。青龙卧墨池、冠世墨玉等都属于黑牡丹一类。青龙卧墨池的雌蕊呈绿色，周围是墨紫色的多层花瓣，似一条青龙盘卧于墨池中央，故称之青龙卧墨池。黑牡丹另外还有泼墨金、乌金耀辉、冠世墨玉、乌紫绒金、深黑紫、瑶池砚墨、墨楼争春等品种。

粉色：粉牡丹温柔娴静，以大金粉、瑶池春最为名贵，其他还有粉丝托桂、春晓、卢氏粉、朱砂葵、粉荷花、粉绣球、粉中冠等。牡丹名贵品种"赵粉"出自清代赵家花园。因花为粉红色而得名，旧时称"童子面"。花型多样，植株生长势强，花量大，为多花品

quickly under sunshine. Therefore, its tissues can be hurt by high temperature, which is not good for the self-protection of flowers. Because of this, natural black peony is quite rare. Another factor that makes black peony rarely seen is that it is hard to develop. Qing Long Wo Mo Chi (green dragon in black lake) and Guan Shi Mo Yu (black jade crowning the world) are both black peonies. The pistil of Qing Long Wo Mo Chi is green and is surrounded by violet black petals, looking like a green dragon in black lake. People therefore give it this name. Other black peony species are Po Mo Jin (black gold), Wu Jin Yao Hui (shining black gold), Wu Zi Rong Jin (dark purple gold), Shen Hei Zi (dark purple), Yao Chi Yan Mo (inkstone of Empres Yao's pond), and Mo Lou Zheng Chun (black peony in spring).

Pink: pink peony flowers look tender and delicate. The most valuable species are Da Jin Fen (golden pink) and Yao Chi Chun (spring of Empress Yao's pond). Others include Fen Si Tuo Gui (pink silk anemone), Chun Xiao (spring dawn), Lu Shi Fen (Lu's pink), Zhu Sha Kui (red sunflower), Fen He Hua (pink lotus), Fen Xiu Qiu (pink silk ball) and Fen Zhong Guan (pink crown). One that worths mentioning is Zhao Fen (Zhao's pink). It was developed by Zhao's family of the Qing Dynasty and was called Tong Zi Mian (child's cheek) because of its pink color. It has strong vitality and numerous varied flowers. Another pink species, Jiu Zui Yang Fei (drunk beauty Yang) has pink lilac flowers with pink top. As the branches are very soft, the flowers lower their heads like drunken beauties. It is therefore called Jiu Zui Yang Fei (drunk beauty Yang).

Multi-color: Multi-color peony flowers refer to peony flowers that have more than two colors in the same flower. Famous ones include: Tian Xiang Zhan Lu (celestial fragrance and clear droplets) and Da Ye Hu Die (big leaf butterfly). The most representative one is Luoyang Jin (Luoyang brocade). It was bred in Yin Li Garden (silk plum) during the reign of Yuan Feng in the Song Dynasty. As its flowers have two different colors, red as bright as fire and white as pure as ice and jade, as if two beautiful ladies competing for better looking, it is also called Er Qiao (two beautiful ladies during the Three Kingdom Period). Multi-color peony usually has purplish red and pink colors in one tree, one branch or even one flower. Luoyang Hong (Luoyang red), also called Zi Er Qiao (purple Er Qiao) or Pu Tong Hong (common red) can grow more than one hundred flowers in a tree. Therefore, it gains the title of new queen of flowers.

Second, the fragrance of flower cannot be neglected. Peony is titled as national flower, not only for its beauty, but also for its fragrance. Praised as

种，清香宜人。另一名贵品种"酒醉杨妃"开粉紫色花，盛开时顶部为粉红色。由于植株枝条柔软，花头下垂，纤纤醉态，故名"酒醉杨妃"。

复色：复色牡丹是指一朵花中不同的花瓣有两种以上不同的颜色，较为名贵的有天香湛露、大叶蝴蝶等。最具代表性的就是洛阳锦，出自宋代元丰年间银李园，因为一花双色，一半红得热烈似火，一半白得冰清玉洁，犹如两位花枝招展的美女争奇斗艳，相得益彰，所以也叫"二乔"。复色牡丹往往同株、同枝可开紫红、粉白两色花朵，或同一朵花上紫红和粉白两色同在，甚为奇特。"洛阳红"又名"紫二乔""普通红"，紫红色，为丰花品种，一株能开百朵花，花繁叶茂，被冠以"新花后"的美称。

其次，要闻花香。牡丹既是国色，也是天香。天香，是花香的最高境界。牡丹花大且美，花香也很馥郁，有"天香""国香""异香""狂香""冷香""馨香"和"第一香"等美誉。一般白色牡丹多香，紫色具烈香，黄粉具清香，只要嗅其香便知其花了。从古到今，诗人对牡丹歌咏最多的，当数一个"香"字。唐代诗人李正封写下"国色朝酣酒，天香夜染衣"，从此"国色天香"成了牡丹的代名词。皮日休一句"竞夸天下无双艳，独占人间第一香"，从此牡丹香列第一。韦庄《白牡丹》诗云："昨夜月明浑似水，入门惟觉一庭香。"花香扑面而来。李山甫《咏牡丹》诗云："数苞仙范火中出，一片异香天上来。"更道出了牡丹花香的奇与异，此香只应天上有，不知何时到人间。也有人称牡丹花香为冷香、馨香、狂香、清香的，体现了诗人对牡丹花香如醉如痴的喜爱。如，薛能《牡丹》诗云："浓艳冷香初盖后，好风乾雨正开

celestial fragrance, it has the highest compliment for flower fragrance. Large, beautiful, and delivering strong and pleasant fragrance, peony flowers are also praised as national fragrance, fantastic fragrance, cold fragrance, pleasant fragrance and the first fragrance. Generally, most white peony flowers smell fragrant. The purple ones have the strongest fragrance and the yellow and pink ones' is gentle. Therefore, you almost can know which species it is just by smelling it. Of all poems on peony, fragrance is what poets mentioned most. Li Zhengfeng of the Tang Dynasty wrote, "Its national beauty intoxicates you in the morning, and its celestial fragrance saturates your clothes in the evening." "National beauty and celestial fragrance" has become another name of peony since then. Pi Rixiu of the Tang Dynasty praised peony that, "No other flowers can compete with it for the beauty, and its fragrance is irreplaceable in the world." In *White Peony*, Wei Zhuang wrote, "Last night's moonlight was as cold and clear as water, when I opened my door, I was perfumed by a gust of fragrance", describing how the fragrance was carried to your face by the wind. Li Shanfu in *Ode to Peony* wrote, "They are celestial flowers growing from fire, with fantastic fragrance coming from heaven", expressing the poet's belief that peony's fragrance is so different that it must be made in heaven. Peony's fragrance is also called cold fragrance, pleasant fragrance and mad fragrance, showing people's zealous love for it. In *Peony*, Xue Neng wrote, "The time when gentle wind blows and light rain falls, they are in full bloom with bright color and cold fragrance amazing visitors."

Qian Guang's *Peony* says, "Its bright color shines with morning dew and its pleasant fragrance flies with wind." Zhuang Huai's *Peony* says, "Among one hundred fragrances sits the god of samadhi (a mental state in Buddhism). Who can find the truth and knowledge from it?" Huang Tingjian in his *Thank Mr. Wang for No.1 Red Peony* says, "The gentle fragrance of peony fills my sleeves, making me feel like being near a shrub of flowers in a famous garden."

Third is flowers' shape. Peony flowers have various shapes. Some of them have whole floral organs, with the sepal, stamen and pistil developing normally, such as Si He Lian (lotus-like peony) and Feng Dan Bai (white phoenix peony). Others stamens and pistils have been vestigial or degenerated into petals, forming various flower shapes. Based on the layer of petals, peony flowers are traditionally divided into three categories: single layer, double layers, and multi-layers. They can also be sub-divided based on the flower shape into sunflower shape, lotus shape, rose shape, hemisphere shape, crown shape, ball shape. This classification can directly reflect the shape variations of flowers. In recent years, peony experts and technicians came up with new classification, based on the traditional classification, their field research and study on peony, and knowledge on the development of different flower shapes: single layer, lotus shape,

时。"谦光《牡丹》云："艳异随朝露，馨香逐晓风。"张淮《牡丹》云："百味狂香三昧神，就中谁解独知真。"黄庭坚《谢王舍人剪送状元红》云："清香拂袖剪来红，似绕名园晓露丛。"

再次，要赏花姿。牡丹花形多变，花态多姿。有的品种，萼片、雄蕊、雌蕊发育正常，如"似荷莲""凤丹白"等；但有的品种雄、雌蕊瓣化或退化，形成了各类风姿绰约的花型。根据花瓣层次的多少，传统上将花分为单瓣（层）类、重瓣（层）类、千瓣（层）类。在这三大类中，又视花朵的形态特征将其分为葵花型、荷花型、玫瑰花型、半球型、皇冠型、绣球型六种花型。这种分类方法比较直观地反映了花朵的各种变化形态。近几年，有关牡丹专家学者与产区的科研人员一起，结合传统的分类方法，经多年实地观察研究及对牡丹花的解剖观察，摸清了花型及花朵构成的演化规律后，提出了新的花型分类，即把牡丹花型分为单瓣型、荷花型、菊花型、蔷薇型、千层台阁型、托桂型、金环型、皇冠型、绣球型、楼子台阁型。

单瓣型：花瓣2～3轮，10～15片，宽大平展，雄蕊200～300个，雌蕊4～6枚，雄、雌蕊发育正常，结实力强。此类花型以"鸦片紫""石榴红""赛珠盘""凤丹白"等品种为代表。

荷花型：花瓣4～5轮，20～25片，花瓣宽大，形状大小近似，排列清晰，雌蕊发育基本正常，结实力较强，但个别品种偶有雄蕊或雌蕊柱头瓣化现象。此类花型以"似荷莲""锦云红""雪莲""玉板白"等品种为代表。

菊花型：花瓣6轮以上，花瓣形状相似，排列整齐，层次分明，自外向内逐

chrysanthemum shape, rose shape, multi-layer pavilion shape, anemone shape, golden ring shape, crown shape, silk ball shape and pavilion shape.

Single layer: two or three layers with ten to fifteen petals. The flower is large and flat with two to three hundred stamens and four to six pistils. Both stamens and pistils grow well and have strong fertility. Peony species of this type include Ya Pian Zi (opium's purple), Shi Liu Hong (pomegranate's red), Sai Zhu Pan (pearl-made tray peony) and Feng Dan Bai (white phenix peony).

Lotus shape: four or five layers with twenty to twenty-five petals. All petals are large, have similar shape and are arranged in order. Pistils are normally developed and have relatively strong fertility. But some species' stamen or pistils have grown to petals. Examples of this type of peony include Si He Lian (lotus-like peony), Jin Yun Hong (rosy cloud), Xue Lian (white lotus) and Yu Ban Bai (jade white).

Chrysanthemum shape: more than six layers with petals of similar sizes arranged orderly layer by layer. From the outside to inside, petals become smaller and smaller. The stamens develop normally or are degraded to smaller ones, some of which have been degenerated into petals. Pistils in one flower total five to eleven, growing normally or being degraded to smaller ones. Some species' pistils are partly changed to petals, having relatively low fertility. Representatives of this type include Mei Gui Hong (rose pink), Cong Zhong Xiao (smile in the shrub of flowers), Yin Hong Qiao Dui (silver with red) and Jin Pao Hong (red brocade).

Rose shape: multi-layer petals becoming smaller from outside to inside. Some stamens are degraded to petals and pistils become smaller or petals, having low fertility. Peony species of this type include Zi Er Qiao (purple beauties), Wu Hua Yao Hui (shining black flowers) and Hong Xia Zheng Hui (red cloud).

Anemone shape: two to five outside petal layers with large petals in order. Some of the stamens are evolved to long and thin petals and the end of petals usually has anther or anther vestige. Normal stamens grow sparsely and irregularly among petals. Pistils are normal or slightly changed to petals, having fertility. Peony species of this type include Shu Nü Zhuang (gentle lady), Jiao Hong (tender red), Xian E (fairy) and San Bian Sai Yu (jade of three styles).

Gold ring shape:two to three petal layers outside with large and flat petals. Some stamens in the heart of flower grow to long and vertical petals and

渐变小，雄蕊正常或退化变小，并偶有瓣化，雌蕊5~11枚，正常生长或退化变小。有些品种柱头有瓣化现象，结实力较差，此类花型以"玫瑰红""丛中笑""银红巧对""锦袍红"等品种为代表。

蔷薇型：花瓣多轮，花瓣由外向内逐渐变小，雄蕊部分瓣化成正常花瓣，雌蕊退化变小或瓣化，结实力差。此类花型以"紫二乔""乌花耀辉""红霞争辉"等品种为代表。

托桂型：外花瓣2~5轮，宽大整齐，部分雄蕊瓣化成细长花瓣，瓣蕊常残留有花药或花药痕迹，瓣间杂有正常雄蕊，排列不规则而稀疏，雌蕊正常或稍有瓣化，具有结实力。此类花型以"淑女装""娇红""仙娥""三变赛玉"等品种为代表。

金环型：外花瓣2~3轮，宽大平展，花朵中心有部分雄蕊瓣化成狭长直立的大花瓣，中心花瓣与外轮花瓣之间有一圈正常雄蕊呈金环状，雌蕊正常或稍有瓣化，结实力差。此类花型极少，以"白天鹅""俊颜红"品种为代表。

皇冠型：外花瓣2～5轮，宽大平展，排列规则，雄蕊大部或全部瓣化成细碎或曲皱花瓣，瓣群稠密耸起，形似皇冠。内花瓣排列不规则，瓣间常杂有正常雄蕊或退化中的雄蕊，瓣端也常残留有花药；雌蕊退化或瓣化，偶有结实。此类花型以"蓝田玉""胡红""姚黄""首案红"等品种为代表。

绣球型：雄蕊充分瓣化，内外瓣形状大小近似，拥挤隆起呈球形或椭圆形；雌蕊基本或全部退化或瓣化，无结实力。此类花型似"豆绿""绿香球""雪映朝霞"等品种为代表。

千层台阁型：下方花瓣4轮以上，花瓣排列

normally developed stamens are between inner and outer petals, like a gold ring. Pistils develop normally or are slightly changed to petals with lower fertility. Peony species of this type are rare, such as Bai Tian E (white swan) and Jun Yan Hong (red face).

Crown shape: two to five outer petal layers with large and flat petals in order. Most or all stamens are evolved to small or crumpled petals, growing together densely like a crown. The inner petals grow irregularly with normal or degraded stamens. The end of petals often has the vestige of anther and pistils develop normally or are partly changed to petals, having low fertility. This type is represented by Lantian Yu (blue jade of Lantian), Hu Hong (Hu's red), Yao Huang (Yao's yellow), and Shou An Hong (Wang Shou An's red).

Silk ball shape: all stamens become petals and all petals have similar shape and size. They crowd together, looking like a ball or an oval. Almost all pistils degrade or become petals, having no fertility. Peony species of this type include Dou Lü (pea's green), Lü Xiang Qiu (green fragrant ball), and Xue Ying Zhao Xia (snow under morning glow).

Multi-layer pavilion shape: more than four layers of lower petals with petals of similar shape arranged in order. Among petals sparsely grow some normal or degraded stamens. The number of normal stamen is small and only a few become petals. Pistils are degraded to smaller one or become petals. The upper petals are less than the lower petals. They are flat or vertical, with stamens and pistils among them degrading to smaller ones. Some pistils are evolved to petals. Peony species of this type include Ling Hua Zhan Lu (flower of water chestnut with clean dew), Zhi Hong (rouge's red), and Shou Xing Hong (the god of longevity's red face).

Pavilion shape: stamens among lower petals become petals, similar to normal ones. Pistils become normal or colorful petals. The upper petals are larger and more than the lower ones in the total number. Almost all stamens degrade or become petals and pistils are evolved to normal or colorful petals among upper petals. Some species' pistils have disappeared. Peony species of this type are Chi Long Ying Cai (red dragon shining), Cheng Dan Lu (stove for golden pills), Yu Lou Dian Cui (jade house on green) and Zi Chong Lou (purple high building).

During the formation of flower shape, some species have two or three or even more shapes in one tree or one branch, such as Zhao Fen (Zhao's pink), Qing Xiang Bai (fragrant green white), Bai He Wo Xue (white crane on snow) and Shan Hua Lan Man (beautiful flowers over mountains). One tree can have flowers of crown shape, Anemone shape, single layer shape and other shapes. The

较整齐，形状近似，瓣间杂有雄蕊和退化的雄蕊。雄蕊正常而量小，或偶有瓣化，雌蕊退化变小或瓣化。上方花瓣量少，平展或直立，雄蕊量少而变小，雌蕊退化变小或瓣化。此类花型以"菱花湛露""脂红""寿星红"等品种为代表。

楼子台阁型：下方花雄蕊瓣化较充分，与正常花瓣形状相似，雌蕊瓣化成正常花瓣或彩瓣。上方花花瓣略大，数量较大，雄蕊基本全部瓣化或退化；雌蕊瓣化成正常花瓣或彩瓣，有的品种退化消失。此类花型以"赤龙焕彩""盛丹炉""玉楼点翠""紫重楼"等品种为代表。

牡丹的花型在演进过程中，有些品种同株、同枝常开两三种花型或更多种花型。如"赵粉""青香白""白鹤卧雪""山花烂漫"等，同株可开"皇冠"、"托桂"、"单瓣型"等花型。所以在确定某一品种的花型时，应以该品种演化达到最高花型为标准。

最后，要品花韵。牡丹株形端庄、花朵硕大、雍容华贵、国色天香、冠绝群芳，被尊为"花王"。千百年来，在国人的心目中，牡丹统领群芳的"花王"地位从未动摇过。对牡丹的欣赏，要从外在美升华到内在美。牡丹既是代表了祥瑞、幸福、贵气的富贵之花，也是传递男女感情的爱情之花。牡丹虽然娇艳，但却不娇气，从野生牡丹分布地域的广泛性与生存条件的巨大差异，我们可以发现牡丹其实出身"贫寒"，在它们身上蕴藏着无限生机。在西南广为分布的黄牡丹，有着相当顽强的适应性和生存能力，它们在干燥、坚硬的红黏土山坡上仍然能够生长、开花、结果！紫斑牡丹在甘肃南部可以分布到海拔近3000米的山地，耐−30℃的低温和严寒。当森林灌丛被大量破坏

classification of these species should be based on the final shape of flowers.

Last but not least is the charm of peony flowers. Peony is praised as the king of flowers for its straight stem, large flower, national beauty and celestial fragrance. This title has been recognized by Chinese people for thousands of years. Chinese people not only appreciate its appearance, but also its inner charm. In their eyes, peony is the symbol of richness, elegance and happiness, as well as the witness of affections for lovers. Though named the king of flowers, it is not a flower of greenhouse. Based on the wide range and great disparity of places where it lives, it is not hard to find that peony has strong vitality and does not require much for the environment. The yellow peony in the southwest part of China almost can grow, bloom and reproduce everywhere, including dry and hard red clay slope. Zi Ban (purple-spot) peony in the south of Gansu Province can live in mountainous areas as high as nearly 3000 meters above sea level and bear cold temperature as low as minus 30 degrees Celsius. Even when the bush wood and forests are destroyed greatly, peony still manages to grow on cliffs. Besides, the Phenix series developed from Yang Shan peony can grow vigorously in the moist and warm south. Peony's strong vitality enables it to live, bloom and reproduce almost in any environment, favorable or adverse. With such beautiful appearance, strong vitality and noble character, no wonder that peony is praised as the national flower representing Chinese culture and spirit.

Peony poetry reading and writing sharing

It's a tradition of Chinese writers to use poems expressing their feelings and make friends through writings. The countless poems and lyrics handed down today show that writing poems while appreciating flowers was very popular in ancient China. Even today people still use poems and lyrics to add joy to festivals. When the first peony festival was held in 1983, Luoyang Literary Federation organized the first Peony Poetry Reading. Since then sharing poems while appreciating peony has become a fixed event during the peony festival.

时，它们在悬崖峭壁上仍努力求得生存。而由杨山牡丹演化而来的"凤丹"系列品种，则能在江南一带湿热环境中健壮生长。在顺境中不娇气，在逆境中不放弃，任何环境里都能开出最灿烂的花朵，不屈不挠，生生不息，有着最美丽的外表、最顽强的生命力和最高尚的品质气节，难怪牡丹能成为代表中华文化与中华民族精神的中国之花。

（二）牡丹诗会、牡丹笔会

以诗传情、以笔会友是中国文人的传统。那流传下来的数不清的与牡丹有关的诗词，证明了千百年前，赏花吟诗已是一种当时广受欢迎的活动。而在现代，人们依旧延续了这一传统活动，用诗歌来装点盛会。1983年，第一届洛阳牡丹花会举办之时，洛阳市文联也正式举办了第一届牡丹诗会，将赏花吟诗变成了牡丹花会上的一项固定的活动。

中国现当代顶尖诗人共赴牡丹诗会。1983年4月15日，洛阳市文联提早筹划牡丹诗会事宜，通过河南省作协和中国作协，向国内的诗坛翘楚遍发英雄帖，邀请他们共赴盛会。一时间，流沙河、牛汉、公刘、严辰、邹荻帆……一批国内顶尖的现代诗人，在牡丹花会开幕后纷至沓来，总数达半百之多，可谓群贤毕至。这些诗人的名字，现今的年轻人或许觉得陌生，但在当时，他们个个都诗名极盛，是那个年代无数文学青年狂热追捧的精神偶像。举个例子，流沙河来洛阳后在原玻璃厂大会堂开讲座，洛阳的诗歌爱好者里三层外三层地围着他要求签名，流沙河深感其诚而来者不拒，最终，这位已到知天命之年的诗人签到手软，累得趴在桌上，还得继续签名……在洛阳期间，这些诗人除了举办讲座和诗歌研讨

Outstanding modern and contemporary Chinese poets gather in Luoyang. on April 15th, 1983, Luoyang Literary Federation started the preparation for Luoyang Poetry Reading and invited famous poets through National Writers Associations and writers associations of provincial level. During the peony festival, more than fifty excellent poets, including Liu Sha He, Niu Han, Gong Liu, Yan Chen, and Zou Difan came to Luoyang. These poets, though might be unfamiliar to today's youths were quite famous for their poems and were regarded as spiritual idols of young man in the bygone era. Take Liu Sha He (Yu Xun Tan) for example, after his arrival in Luoyang, Yu gave a speech in the hall of Luoyang Glass Factory. Poetry lovers in Luoyang swarmed around him and asked for his autograph. Impressed by their sincerity, Yu did not have the heart to turn them down. In the end, this fifty-year-old poet was so tired that he had to bend over his desk to write. When in Luoyang, besides giving lectures and participating in poetry symposiums, these poets appreciated peony flowers and visited many places of interests, having a great time. After they left Luoyang, many of them voluntarily sent their poems on experiences in Luoyang to the literary federation. The total 43 poems were published on *Peony* in July and August, 1983. By describing Luoyang peony, Longmen Grottoes, Guan Lin Temple, tri-coloured glazed potteries of the Tang Dynasty, Luoyang Bearing Factory, Bai Juyi's tomb, and the place where great poets Li Bai and Du Fu met, they made Luoyang more poetic and famous in China.

At that time, the reform and opening up policy had been conducted for only a few years and there was almost no national poetry sharing activities. Therefore, when peony poetry reading was held in Luoyang, it got great attention, achieving huge success and becoming a major event for Chinese poets. Since then, this activity or similar event has been held every year during the peony festival and many famous poets and writers like Ye Yanbing, Han Zuorong, Lin Ran, Hai Nan and Zeng Zhuo came on invitation. Some of them were born in Luoyang and were very glad to express their love for hometown when they got back after many years. Later, the fame of peony poetry reading was even heard across Taiwan Strait. Many excellent Taiwan poets, especially those who have emotional bond

会外, 还忙里偷闲, 得以赏花游城。离洛之后, 许多诗人都主动交上了自己的一份作业——把他们的游洛经历和感受写成诗作寄来, 总数达43首, 集中发表在1983年7—8月号的《牡丹》上, 诗文内容涉及洛阳牡丹、龙门石窟、关林、唐三彩、洛阳轴承厂、白居易墓、李白杜甫相会处……生花妙笔, 把个洛阳城渲染得诗意盎然, 也让这个城市声名远播。

彼时的中国, 改革开放还没几个年头, 全国性的诗歌笔会活动先前几乎从没有过, 因此, 牡丹诗会在那年一问世, 就受到了极大关注, 取得了极大成功, 成为当时中国诗坛的一大盛事。此后, 洛阳年年都要在牡丹花会期间举办牡丹诗会或者类似的诗歌笔会活动, 叶延滨、韩作荣、林染、海男、曾卓等众多的诗坛名家先后应邀而来, 还有不少洛阳籍的一流诗人, 在离洛多年后重归故土, 再叙乡情。再往后，牡丹诗会的名头甚至传到了海峡对岸，许多享有盛誉的台湾诗人，尤其是当地那些与河洛文化有着深厚渊源的著名诗人，也不远千里赶赴牡丹之约，将一般人眼中的以诗会友的闲情逸致，升华为血脉相连、共望统一的中华情。

难舍黄土黄河水。

牡丹诗会的名声传到了宝岛台湾，成为许多台湾诗人与大陆交流的桥梁和纽带，高雄市文协秘书长潘雷就是亲历者之一。潘雷祖籍河南荥阳，一生诗作颇丰，在台湾诗坛享有盛誉。1999年4月21日，已是七旬老人的潘雷首回大陆，第一站到的就是洛阳。在迫不及待地踏上洛阳的土地后，他说的第一句话是："终于到家了！"原来，在老先生的心灵深处，一直秉承古代的行政区划，将荥阳认可为洛阳辖区，而把自己当做"河洛人"。但潘雷那一年来得有些晚了，王城公园的牡丹园中只剩下一

with Heluo culture, went to Luoyang despite the thousand-mile distance. This changed the traditional recreational activity to a bridge that links both sides of Taiwan Strait, expressing their wish for reunification.

Loath to part with the homeland and Yellow River. After peony poetry reading got known in Taiwan, it became a bridge for exchanges between poets in the mainland and Taiwan. Pan Lei, secretary of Gao Xiong Writers Association of Taiwan witnessed this change. His ancestral home is Xingyang, Henan. Having written a lot of poems during his life, Pan had a high reputation among poets of Taiwan. When this seventy-year-old man got back to the mainland for the first time in April 21st, 1999, his first destination was Luoyang. After he finally stepped on the land of Luoyang, his first word was "finally home." For him, Xingyang is part of Luoyang based on the traditional classification and he considers himself should be a local of Heluo district. The pity is that by the time he arrived, all peony flowers in Wangcheng Park had withered and fell, leaving green branches waiting for next year's bloom. Unable to appreciate peony flower, Pan felt very sad. His friends comforted him in the welcome dinner that, "Peony flowers bloom every year. If you come earlier next year, you will not miss it.

This time, we will take you to the famous Longmen Grottoes and the Xiaolangdi Reservoir. I am sure that you will enjoy your time here." He nodded and emptied his cup in one quaff.

The next day, Pan visited all places of interests in Luoyang and his last destination was the bank of Yellow River on the north of the city. At sunset, when a poet of Luoyang was telling the story of eight hundred dukes meeting in Mengjin, Pan suddenly ran towards the Yellow River. He squatted to gently hold water in both hands and then drank all the water in one draught. When he stood up, people nearby could see his eyes full of teardrops. When he was leaving Luoyang for Zhengzhou Airport, Pan suddenly yelled to the driver, "Stop! Stop the car." But they were in the expressway and where could the driver park the car? Knowing that this old man came from Taiwan, the driver managed to park in a resting area. Pan quickly got off the car and tried to stride over the one-meter tall rail, but he failed after several trials. Knowing his intention, Pan's friend strode over the rail, ran towards the field, put

处处碧绿的阔叶，所有的牡丹已经开始孕育下一个春天了。无缘见到牡丹，潘雷深以为憾，洛阳的诗友在接风宴上安慰他说："洛阳牡丹年年开放，您明年稍微早来几天就好了。这一回，我们带您去看看闻名天下的龙门，看看马上就要实现大河截流的小浪底工程……保证让您不虚此行。"潘雷点点头，将杯中酒一饮而尽。

次日全天，潘雷遍游洛阳，最后一站往北出了市区，来到黄河岸边。在夕阳的映照中，洛阳的诗友讲述起八百诸侯会孟津的历史故事，潘雷突然向黄河水边跑去。只见他轻轻地蹲下，小心翼翼地用双手捧起黄河水，急切地啜饮起来。当他一口气饮干手中的黄河水立起身时，人们看到他眼中闪动着泪光……在恋恋不舍地离开洛阳时，汽车刚刚驶上前往郑州机场的高速公路，坐在后排座上的潘雷突然叫了起来："师傅，停车、停车！"高速公路上怎能随便停车？司机好生为难，但得知老先生是台湾同胞后，把车靠边慢慢停了下来。潘雷急匆匆地走下车，想跨过路边1米高的护栏，但跨了几下没能过去。洛阳的诗友对他的意图心领神会，跨过护栏，跑到路边的田野，拨开田垄上的碎石，把双手深深地插入湿润的土壤中……当这位诗友把一捧黄土放到潘雷早已准备好的一块大大的手帕里时，老先生就像捧着祖先的牌位一样，孩子似的哭了起来……潘雷说，他要把这些黄土带回台湾去。他还说，这次错过了牡丹花期，他非常遗憾，请洛阳的诗友回头给他寄一些牡丹种子，他要让洛阳牡丹在祖国的宝岛上盛开。

the stones apart and dug a handful of soil. When he put the soil on the handkerchief Pan had prepared, Pan cried like a baby, as if he was holding the memorial tablet of ancestors. He said that he would take the soil to Taiwan and he felt very sorry to miss the flowering period of peony. He asked poets in Luoyang to send him the seeds of peony, so that peony flowers could bloom in Taiwan.

Having five bowls of noodles in succession.
Li Laoxiang's name is as strange as his nickname:
West Eccentric Poet. (Laoxiang in Chinese means
fellow-villager). He was not only the editor and
reviser of *Fei Tian* (Flying Apsaras), a monthly
magazine of Gansu, but also the vice president of
Writers Association of Gansu Province. Having
received the Excellent Poem Reward of the Third
Lu Xun Literary Prize, Li was titled as the Chaplin
poet. The most worth mentioning part is that he was
born in Yichuan, north of Luoyang. He attended the
peony poetry reading of the 13th peony festival in
April, 1995. Not having been back for a long time,
Li still had Luoyang accent and his hair had been
white. During his visit in Luoyang, Li recalled his
past experiences in Luoyang and was amazed by the
city's changes.

On the way to an old temple outside Luoyang,
they saw a vendor selling noodles on the road side.
Li immediately went to him and wanted to have
a taste. There were only less than half barrel of
noodles. All people accompanying him asked for
one bowl, so did Li. But he quickly finished his
and asked for one more. He asked for one more
again and again, until all noodles were eaten up. He
altogether had five bowls of noodles in an incredible
speed, amazing all people there. "No one ever
thought that such a fifty year old, thin man could eat

连吃五碗浆面条。李
老乡的名字挺怪，就像他
的外号——"西部诗怪"
一样。这位诗坛名家，不
仅当过甘肃《飞天》文学
月刊编审和甘肃省作协副
主席，获得过第三届鲁迅
文学奖全国优秀诗歌奖，
被誉为"一个卓别林式的
喜剧诗人"，而且最重要
的是，他还真是一位从伊
川县走出去的老乡。1995
年4月第13届牡丹花会，
洛阳再办牡丹诗会，李老
乡借此机会，终于回到了
阔别已久的家乡。乡音无
改鬓毛衰，在洛阳赏花游
城、访古寻幽的路上，李
老乡一次次触动乡情，感
慨连连。

在去洛阳郊外一处
古庙的路上，见路边有一
小贩正在叫卖浆面条，李
老乡当即犯了馋瘾，直奔
小贩而去。小贩的木桶中
只余小半桶浆面条了，几
名陪同者一人吃了一碗，
李老乡也要了一碗，"稀
里哗啦"几口就吃完了，
接着他要了第二碗，很快
就又吃完了，然后他又要

了第三碗……直到木桶见底，他一连吃了五碗浆面条，每一碗吃得都是狼吞虎咽，将在场人惊得目瞪口呆！谁能想到，这么个干干瘦瘦、年过半百之人，居然这么能吃！李老乡吃下五碗浆面条后，双手拍拍肚子，用一种心满意足的口吻说："痛快！就是这个味儿……"浓浓的乡情，溢于言表。

直把牡丹作假花。提起四川诗人流沙河，很多人都能想起他那首入选过中学语文课本的名作——《就是那一只蟋蟀》。1983年4月，这位少年时代就因才识扬名的一流诗人，欣然赶赴首届牡丹诗会。那是流沙河生平头一回来到洛阳，彼时，他已是年过半百之人。来洛阳的诗人们到王城公园观赏牡丹，流沙河也在其中。目睹了洛阳牡丹的芳姿后，这些平素极富想象力的诗人，对眼前的国色天香之美无不感到不可思议，以至于浑然忘我。尤其是流沙河，表情和眼神

this much." Qiao said. After having five bowls of noodle, Li patted his belly and said with satisfaction, "Yes! This is the taste that I remembered", showing his deep lovesickness for hometown.

Regarding peony as fake flowers. Hearing the name of Liu Sha He, people might think of his famous poem selected in middle school textbook, It is *That Cricket*. He became well known for his gift when he was still young and participated the first Peony Poetry Reading in April, 1983. It was his first time to Luoyang and he was around fifty years old. Mei Yixin remembers that during the peony festival, he accompanied Liu Sha He and other poets to appreciate peony flowers in Wangcheng Park. Seeing the beautiful peony flowers, though these poets had wild imaginations, they were totally amazed by the national beauty and celestial fragrance, losing themselves in the beauty of flowers. Liu Sha He's shock could be clearly seen from his face and eyes. He kept murmuring, "So large, so bright, and so beautiful! Just like the fake flowers on paintings. Are they fake? Otherwise how come they look exactly like the ones painted or man-made? Such

beauty indeed exists!" His words clearly showed his surprise and satisfaction of seeing the flowers that should only exist in heaven and people on earth could rarely see.

Peony calligraphy works and painting exhibitions

Poetry and paintings can not be separated in China. Besides using words to express feeling, Chinese people also like to use paintings to record the bloom of peony flowers and show their love towards peony. During every peony festival, peony calligraphy works and painting exhibitions in Luoyang Museum, Luoyang Gallery, and exhibition halls, attract many citizens and visitors to experience and appreciate peony art.

During the 28th Peony Cultural Festival in 2010, Painting Exhibition of Six Alumni from China Central Academy of Fine Arts (CAFA) was

里写满了惊愕，口中还止不住地念叨："太大了，太艳了，太美了! 跟我从前在画上见过的洛阳牡丹一模一样! 这些花该不是假的吧? 要不然，它们的花形和花色怎么可能和画出来或者做出来的牡丹完全一样? 这天地之间，难道还真有此等绝色……"言中之意，深为洛阳牡丹所折服，大有"此花只应天上有，人间哪得几回闻"之满足感。

（三）牡丹书画展

诗画不分家，除了用文字来传递感情，人们也喜欢用笔和画来记录牡丹的每一分舒展，表达自己对于牡丹的喜爱。每一年的牡丹花会都会有不少牡丹书画作品在洛阳博物馆、美术馆、展览厅等地进行展出，吸引了不少市民和游客前来欣赏，从中体会艺术化了的牡丹文化。

2010年第28届洛阳牡丹花会期间，"中央美术学院同窗六人画展"在洛阳美

术馆举办，画家寇衡、武海鹰、于大武、扈庚成、史殿生、米洪江六人也到会与大家见面。他们参展的共有六十幅作品，展示了中央美院学院派艺术风格。与此同时还举办了"寇衡、寇莹唐诗工笔画展"，这是洛阳市著名画家寇衡与女儿寇莹历经数年，艰辛创作的工笔画版的唐诗、宋词。与朗朗上口的著名诗词相对应的工笔画，显示出清丽脱俗的画风，反映了作者对古诗词文化的深刻理解，人物刻画细腻，栩栩如生，构思巧妙，意境深远，具有较高的艺术水准。另外，同时在洛阳美术馆展览的还有意象水墨画展、当代名家牡丹画邀请展、河南省首届农民画大展等多种展览。为广大书画爱好者送上了丰盛的精神大餐。

2011年第29届洛阳牡丹文化节期间，由中共洛阳市委宣传部、洛阳市文化广电新闻出版局、洛阳市文联主办，洛阳市美术家协会、洛阳书画院、洛阳博物馆

held in Luoyang Gallery. The six painters, Kou Heng, Wu Haiying, Yu Dawu, Hu Gengcheng, Shi Diansheng and Mi Hongjiang came to Luoyang and met viewers. Their sixty paintings demonstrated the academicism style of CAFA. Kou Heng and Kou Ying Gongbi (elaborate-style) Paintings of Tang poems were also exhibited during that time. Concentrated by years' efforts of Kou Heng and his daughter, and accompanied with well-known poems and lyrics, these paintings looked refined and elegant. Besides, because of painters' profound understanding, elaborate and lively depiction of figures, and creative designs, the paintings had deep meanings and high artistic values. Luoyang Gallery also held. The Image Wash Painting Exhibition, Outstanding Contemporary Peony Painting Exhibition, and The First Farmer Painting Show of Henan Province, offering a spiritual feast for paintings and calligraphy lovers.

During the 29th Peony Cultural Festival in 2011, Luoyang Outstanding Peony Painting Exhibition, hosted by the publicity department of Luoyang Municipal Party Committee, Luoyang Municipal Bureau of Culture, Radio, TV and Publication, and Luoyang Literary Federation, and organized by Luoyang Artists Association, Luoyang Institute of Calligraphy and Paintings, and Luoyang Museum, was held in Luoyang Museum. More than one hundred paintings of different contents, styles, forms and schools were shown there, lively manifesting the beauty, elegance and dignity of peony. This exhibition presented the whole ability of peony painters, the latest peony works, and deep peony culture of Luoyang, with the most peony painters participating and the best peony paintings among all peony painting exhibitions. Both famous painters including Wang Xiu, Wen Liuchuan, Xie Jinfeng, Zhao Dongjun, Kou Heng, Gao Shaohua, Suo Tiesheng and Zhang Jianjing, and up-and-coming painters like Wang Xia, Li Lan and Li Yong exhibited their works, representing the highest level of peony paintings in Luoyang. This exhibition played an important role in enhancing Luoyang culture, adding more artistic beauty to the festival, boosting the prosperity of peony paintings and offering a good platform for painting lovers to exchange their views.

Besides Outstanding Peony Painting Exhibition in old Luoyang Museum, during the peony cultural

承办的洛阳牡丹画精品展在洛阳博物馆举办，共展出洛阳市牡丹画作者的精品佳作百余幅，内容丰富，形式多样，或奇或正，或工或写，或泼墨或赋彩，可谓异彩纷呈，生动地表现出牡丹的娇艳姿容、华贵的气质和典雅的品格，集中展示了洛阳牡丹画作品的群体实力，洛阳牡丹画派的最新成果和洛阳牡丹文化的深厚底蕴。这次展览是洛阳市历次牡丹画展中参展画家最多、作品技艺最精湛的一次大展，其中有王绣、文柳川、解金峰、赵东军、寇衡、高少华、索铁生、张建京等洛阳市著名画家的上乘佳作，也有近几年脱颖而出的王霞、李兰、李勇等一批画坛新秀的新人作品，代表了洛阳市牡丹画创作的最高水平。此展为提升洛阳的文化品位，为第29届中国洛阳牡丹文化节增添了靓丽的艺术风采，也为洛阳市牡丹画作者相互切磋技艺，促进牡丹画创作的进一步繁荣提供了平台。

除洛阳博物馆老馆的洛阳牡丹画精品展外，牡丹节期间，洛阳美术馆、洛阳博物馆新馆、平乐牡丹画创意园区也有多场书画展展出。美术馆举办了"西望长安——四人中国画展""兰亭汇——第三届中国书法奖洛阳作者作品联展""全国第二届线描画获奖作品展""洛阳新乡书画联展""郭朝卿、李新国牡丹书画联展"和"洛阳市首届青年书画展"等一系列画展。"全国牡丹画学术邀请展"和"全国农民画展"在孟津平乐牡丹画创意园区举行。此外，"洛神春赋——何水法画展"在洛阳博物馆新馆举行。这一系列的书画展览，为洛阳广大市民以及来洛阳观赏牡丹和古都旅游的中外来宾奉上了丰盛的文化大餐。

而在2012年第30届中国洛阳牡丹文化节上，展出了一幅《千姿百态千米长卷牡丹图》，并申请吉尼斯世界纪录。这幅围绕"国运昌则花运昌"的主题，面向全国征集牡丹作品，历时一年，最终选出了1300幅牡丹图画制成千米长卷，让牡丹"美

festival, there were also many shows held in Luoyang Gallery, the new building of Luoyang museum, and Pingle Creative Peony Painting Zone. Look Westward: Xi' an — Chinese Paintings from Four Painters, Lan Ting Exhibition — Group Exhibitions of Rewarded Calligraphers in the Third Chinese Calligraphy Competition, Rewarded Works Exhibition of the Second National Line Drawing Competition, Co-exhibition of Calligraphy Works and Paintings from Luoyang and Xinxiang, Co-exhibition of Guo Chaoqin and Li Xinguo's Peony Paintings and Calligraphy Works, and The First Luoyang Young Calligraphers and Painters' Works Exhibition were held in Luoyang Gallery. Pingle Creative Peony Paintings Zone in Mengjin organized National Peony Painting Exhibition and National Farmer Painting Show. And the new building of Luoyang Museum held Spring Ode to the Goddess of Luo River—He Shuifa Works Exhibition. These exhibitions formed a great cultural festival for Luoyang citizens and visitors from home and abroad who came to appreciate peony and visited Luoyang.

During the 30th Peony Cultural Festival in 2012, a one-thousand-meter-long Peony Map with All Sorts of Stances was shown in Luoyang and created a new Guinness record. Themed as "prosperous China with blooming peony", it collected peony paintings nationwide. After one year's effort, the organizing committee picked one thousand three hundred peony paintings to create a one-thousand-meter picture with various peony flowers blooming, which expressed painters' wish for the prosperity of China. By depicting various and gorgeous peony flowers, the Peony Map with All Sorts of Stances made viewers learn the history of calligraphy and painting, feel moving love stories and legends, and experience the historical changes of China and showed the rich Chinese culture.

Among all exhibitions, the most distinctive one is Pingle Farmer Painting Exhibition in Mengjin. Praised as China's first peony painting village, Pingle village in Mengjin county has many farmers starting painting peony as an entertainment activity during the slack season in the 1980s. This activity later was gradually developed into an industry with more than one hundred professional peony painters and four hundred farmer painters producing more than one hundred thousand paintings every year. Their works not only received great attention during the festival but also were shown in Pingle Farmer Peony Paintings and Luoyang Outstanding Peony Works Exhibition in 798 Art Zone of

人"与历史"英雄"来一场跌宕起伏的华丽共舞。不仅更以此来庆贺祖国的繁荣昌盛和兴旺发达。《千姿百态千米长卷牡丹图》是一场视觉盛宴，让观者通过欣赏形态各异，风姿迥异的牡丹花了解书画艺术的发展演变，感受缠绵悱恻的爱情传奇，体会中国历史的沧桑巨变，展现了中华民族丰厚的文化底蕴。

在这些画展中，尤为有特色的是孟津县平乐镇农民画家画展系列。被誉为"中国牡丹画第一村"的孟津县平乐村，自20世纪80年代初以来，农民们在农忙之余，开始追求文化艺术，于是执笔画牡丹，逐渐将其发展为一种产业，现有百余个牡丹画专业户和400多名农民画师，年创作生产牡丹画10万余幅。平乐农民画展不仅在节日中受到关注与好评，更于2010年在北京798艺术区举办了中国平乐农民牡丹画暨洛阳牡丹艺术精品展，使洛阳牡丹文化节的影响扩展到了首都北京。此次展览上，360多幅农民创作的富丽大气的牡丹画，上百件造型独特、制作精良的洛阳唐三彩、奇石、青铜器、澄泥砚、麦秸画作品，把2500多平方米的展厅装扮得绚丽夺目，吸引了包括全国两会代表、委员在内的千余各界人士和中外游客参观。展览上，30位农民画师身着统一的红色唐装，现场作画。画师郭西凡说："进京办展览，使我们深受鼓舞，将对我们提高技艺起到促进作用。"色彩绚丽、技法日趋纯熟的平乐农民牡丹画，受到参观者的极大关注。广州美院教授、著名画家周彦生说，现在在洛阳画牡丹的仅农民就有这么多，水平也很高，说明洛阳牡丹文化真正得到了发扬光大。来自法国阿尔萨斯的李木夫妇还当场向一位农民画师学画牡丹。李木说，这些画色彩鲜艳，非常特别，中国农民画家的创作技艺让他佩服和欣赏。

Beijing, enlarging their influence and fame. On the exhibition, more than 360 peony paintings, and more than one hundred unique and refined handicraft works including peony stones, bronze wares, Chengni inkstones, wheat straw pictures and tri-coloured glazed potteries of the Tang Dynasty made by farmers decorated the 2500-square-meter exhibition hall, attracting one thousand-odd viewers, including members of National People's Congress (NPC), members of Chinese People's Political Consultative Conference (CPPCC) and visitors from China and abroad. 30 farmer painters wearing uniform Tang suit, painted on the scene. Guo Xifan, one of the painters said, "The exhibition in Beijing greatly encouraged us and will further improve our drawings." These bright and more and more refined farmer paintings draw great attention. Zhou Yansheng, a famous painter and professor of Guangzhou Academy of Fine Arts, said that these abundant and outstanding farmers peony painting showed that Luoyang peony culture had been greatly promoted and popularized. A couple from Alsace, France learned how to draw peony from one of the farmer painters on site. The husband, Li Mu said that these painting had bright color and unique style. He really admired and appreciated these farmers' painting skills.

Peony lantern show

Lantern show is an important folk custom and cultural activity in China. Lantern show in Luoyang, the birth land of Chinese civilization, has a very long history and enjoys high reputation. "Appreciating peony in the day and lantern show in the night" is a tradition of Luoyang peony festival. As time goes by, lantern show has gained new content and is vitalized again. With the holding of peony culture festival, lantern show has been held for thirty times. Thanks to the large participation of enterprises, institutes, organizations, associations and citizens in Luoyang, it gradually becomes a large cultural event with mass participation. Its influence is still increasing and its quality is improved. Every April when the blooming peony flowers' fragrance is all over Luoyang, colorful lanterns shine like stars. They enhance the beauty of sunset glow and lighten the dark sky in the night, relaxing visitors and making them too delighted to leave.

While inheriting traditional craftsmanship, lantern makers introduce modern photoelectricity technology and learn from other arts, integrating

（四）牡丹灯会

彩灯文化是我国民间一项重要的传统习俗和文化活动。作为华夏文明发源地的古都洛阳，彩灯文化更是源远流长，久负盛名。"昼赏牡丹夜观灯"更是洛阳牡丹花会的老传统了。而随着时代步伐的不断前进，灯事活动又被赋予了新的内容，这一古老的民间艺术瑰宝又焕发了青春。随着牡丹花会一年一度的举办，洛阳牡丹灯会活动也至30届了。由于洛阳市各大厂矿企业、事业单位、科研院所的积极参与，广大市民的大力支持，灯会逐渐成为洛阳一项群众性的大型文化活动，灯会规模越办越大，活动越办越好。每年阳春三月，牡丹盛开，满城飘香的时候，一盏盏彩灯喷吐出万道光焰，染红漫天流霞，摇醉寂静夜空，令人流连忘返。

洛阳彩灯在继承传统制灯工艺的基础上，引进了现代光电技术，吸取了其他艺术门类的营养，集声、色、光、动、型为一体，熔观赏性、趣味性、知识性于一炉，逐步形成了锦绣中华、名胜古迹、历史典故、国花牡丹、民俗风情五大彩灯系列。那一组组彩灯造型各异、色彩斑斓，规模之壮观，运转之灵活，制作之精美，令人赞叹。

　　2008年第26届洛阳牡丹灯会。这一届洛阳牡丹灯会的灯饰主要是从元宵节灯展中选取一些有代表性的、能够体现制作者匠心的优秀作品，并在元宵节灯展作品基础上有所创新。因为2008年是中国举办奥运会之年，所以神态各异、活灵活现的奥运福娃是此次灯展的最大亮点，吸引着广大游客前来与福娃们合影。福娃主要有用不同颜色的LED灯带盘绕而成和以白炽灯在内部衬托的布艺制作这两种方式。动画片《猫和老鼠》中这对冤家没有终结的追逐和打闹也深受欢迎，森林之王、白雪公主

sound, appearance, light, movement and style together to offer visitors an interesting, enjoyable and educational experience. They create five series of lanterns: splendid China, places of interests, historical stories, peony, and folk customs. These lanterns' various shapes, bright colors, flexible movement, refined structures and large size amazed many viewers.

　　The 26th peony lantern show in 2008: lanterns of this festival were mainly chosen from the lantern show of lantern festival. Representative and original, they were added with some innovations. Since Beijing held the 29th Olympic Games in 2008, the most popular ones were lovely and vivid mascots, attracting many visitors to take picture with them. These mascots lanterns were made by surrounding different colors of LED light rope around the cloth and putting incandescent bulb inside. Lanterns on Tom and Jerry's never-end fight and play from the popular cartoon also drew many people's attention. Besides, many characters of cartoons and fairy tales such as the king of forest, Snow White and Seven Dwarfs were presented in the form of lanterns. The lantern show not only showed the history of lanterns, but also integrated traditional culture. Every lantern had related introduction, helping visitors learn Chinese culture and understand the origin and development of lanterns while appreciating the beauty of lanterns. The appearance of both traditional and modern lanterns astonished visitors by their refined craftsmanship and fast development.

The 28th peony lantern show in 2010: as the venue of 28th peony lantern show, Wangcheng Park arranged thirty-five groups of lanterns with different contents and themes. "This year's lantern show mainly focuses on presenting local features and highlighting the elements of Luoyang and Wangcheng," one manager of Wangcheng Park said. When people walked into the park, the first thing they saw was a peony lantern screen, sixteen meters high and five meters wide with various artificial peony flowers blooming on it. Beside the Peony Fairy was National Flower lantern. All the man-made flowers on it were very delicate and lovely as if real. The opening ceremony of the First Luoyang Peony Festival was held in Peony Pavilion of

和七个小矮人等家喻户晓的动画片和童话书中的人物以灯饰的形式展现在人们面前。此次灯展不仅体现了彩灯的发展，也将传统文化融入其中。每个灯展作品旁边还配有相关的解说，让游客在看灯展的同时学习中国文化。还有介绍灯的起源及其发展，将古代到现代有代表性的灯饰展现在人们面前，让人不得不惊叹灯饰发展的迅速和其制造的精巧。

2010年第28届洛阳牡丹灯会。作为第28届洛阳牡丹灯会的举办地点，王城公园早就被安装了35组内容丰富、题材多样的彩灯。此届灯会主打"本地牌"，着力突出洛阳元素、王城特色。一走进公园正门，映入眼帘的便是"牡丹灯屏"：在高16米、宽5米的屏风上，姹紫嫣红的"牡丹"竞相绽放；"牡丹仙子"彩灯旁边，"国花牡丹"朵朵精致，"争芳吐艳"吸人眼球。1983年，第一届洛阳牡丹花会开幕式在王城公园牡丹阁举行。20多年过去了，昔日的牡丹阁已不复存在。技术人员用彩灯按牡丹阁的形制做出"牡丹阁"灯组，该组彩灯极具纪念价值和观赏价值。再看华南虎题材的彩灯，在大型灯组"虎山"上，"虎妞妞""虎亮亮"带着它们的孩子"华华""南南""虎虎""旺旺"和"虎妞"玩闹嬉戏，令人忍俊不禁。

2011年第29届洛阳牡丹灯会。此届牡丹灯会共计布置彩灯42组。其中，将展出"中国馆""武后赏花""马寺钟声""春天的故事"等大型彩灯16组，"中国腾飞""祖国万岁"等中小型彩灯26组，机械灯组22组，宫灯和满天星等装饰类彩灯2000余盏。灯会更加突出"牡丹"的主题，展出的彩灯以大型灯为主。除此之外，还有微缩的世博会"中国馆"、活灵活现的"华南虎旺家族"以及充满童趣的"喜洋洋""动物世界"等大中型彩灯，营造出灯光幻影的海洋。

Wangcheng Park in 1983. After more than twenty years, the pavilion no longer existed. Technicians created a series of Peony Pavilion lanterns based on its original shape, which were very memorable and valuable. There was another group of lanterns themed as South China Tiger. On the Tiger Hill, Niuniu and Liangliang were playing with their children Huahua, Nannan, Huhu, Wangwang and Huniu. Their lovely appearances and postures made visitors could not help laughing.

The 29th peony lantern show in 2011: there were altogether 42 groups of lanterns, including sixteen large ones such as China Pavillion, Empress Wu Appreciating Flowers, Bell of Baima Temple and The Story of Spring, twenty-six small and medium-sized colored ones such as The Leap of China, and Long Live China. There were also twenty-two groups of mechanical lights and more than two thousand decorative lights like palace lanterns and starry lights. The lantern show in 2011 highlighted the theme "peony" and mainly exhibited large lanterns. Gorgeous China Pavilion, lifelike South China Tiger, lovely Xi Yangyang (a character of a famous Chinese cartoon), and wonderful Animal World provided visitors a sea of lights.

Folk fair

Folk fair is a very popular traditional folk activity in China. Also named folk market and festival fair, it was usually held near temples. During the fair, people nearby get together, offering sacrifice to god or ancestors, amusing themselves through entertainment and doing some shopping. Folk fair is a traditional activity of the Luoyang peony festival. Every year organizers exhibit many important symbols of Heluo culture, such as Luoyang bass drum and disk drum, and Luoyang intangible cultural heritages like Two Ghosts Wrestling, puppet show, and lion dance to help visitors from home and abroad understand Heluo culture better. Besides, various folk works of art like tri-colored glazed potteries of the Tang Dynasty, Chengni inkstones, dough sculptures, clay sculptures, wood carvings, pyrographs, sugar sculptures, root carvings, fabrics works, grass paintings, grotesque stones, paper-cut works, bronze reliefs and bronze ware are all displayed, amazing many visitors. As time goes, venues of folk fair are no longer limited to traditional markets. Museums, Cultural Palace and other places take part in it, adding painting exhibitions and art shows and enriching the folk fair.

（五）民俗文化庙会

庙会是中国民间广为流传的一种传统民俗活动，又称"庙市"或"节场"，一般是指在寺庙附近聚会，进行祭神、娱乐和购物等活动。民俗文化庙会是洛阳牡丹花会的一项传统文化旅游活动，每届都会集中展示一批河洛地区的民俗文化，已经成为中外游客了解河洛文化的重要文化品牌，如洛阳大鼓、盘鼓，入选洛阳市非物质文化遗产项目的二鬼摔跤、木偶戏、舞狮等。除此之外，唐三彩、澄泥砚、面塑、泥塑、陶艺、木雕、烙画、糖塑、根艺、布艺、麦草画、奇石、剪纸、铜浮雕、青铜器等各种民间艺术品的展示也让游客们啧啧称奇。随着时代的发展，洛阳民俗文化庙会的地点也扩充到博物馆、文化宫等场所，增加了画展、艺术展等不同类型的活动，使得庙会的内容更加丰富。

2008年第18届洛阳民俗文化庙会。在这一届民俗文化庙会上，洛宁县城关镇当竹女子大鼓、盘鼓队为大家进行了表演。在五名六七岁女孩的大鼓引领下，数十名身穿节日盛装的成人队员打镲击铙，奏出慷慨激昂的强音。紧接着亮相的是偃师市府店镇参驾店狮舞团，这是一个有着百余年历史的民间文艺表演团体。台上，巾帼英豪们扮演的雄狮精神抖擞，英姿飒爽。一位八旬老太太队员步履矫健，身轻如燕，令观众赞叹。来自陕西省宝鸡县赤沙镇"快活社火"所表演的节目也让洛阳观众大开眼界。这是陕西乃至全国唯一保留的一个社火种类，以《水浒传》中武松杀西门庆为其兄武大郎报仇的故事为素材，表演内容为斧子、剪刀、镰刀、锥子等器具刺入西门庆和其他坏人头部。取名"快活"的意思是：《水浒传》中的地名为"快活林"；铲除了为非作歹的恶人后人心快活。除表演以外，民

The 18th Luoyang folk fair in 2008: Dang Zhu Female Bass Drum and Dick Drum Team of Cheng Guan town, Luo Ning county was the first to give performance in the folk fair. Under the lead of drums played by five six to seven years old girls, dozens of adult performers dressed in their holiday attires, played small cymbals and big cymbals, making powerful and exciting sound. After them was the lion dance team from Canjia Dian village, Fudian town, Yanshi city. This teams was established more than one hundred years ago and the lions performed by these women were all energetic and valiant. One member in the team was more than eighty years old, but her walk was as agile as that of a swallow, impressing a lot of audience. The performance of Happy She Huo (She Huo is a traditional drama performed during festivals in the west of China) from Chisha, Baoji, Shaanxi province was also an eye-opener. As the only retained She Huo drama in Shaanxi and even China, it was about how Wu Song killed Ximen Qing to revenge his dead brother. Performers used axes, scissors, sickles and awls to hit Ximen Qing and other villains' heads. The name "Happy" came from the place called Happy Forest in *All Men Are Brothers*, a popular fiction by Shi Nai'an, showing people's applause after the villains were killed. Besides performances, Luoyang Folk Museum prepared several folk activities for visitors: Jiang Ziya's braid exhibition, Tian Tian Le Pet Show from Yanshi, Luoshan shadow show, dough figures making, and paper-cut works of pupils. During the folk fair, citizens and visitors could also watch the procedure of making dough sculptures and sugar sculptures, and visit paper-cut works exhibition and Lu's wood engraving pictures show.

The 20th Luoyang folk fair in 2010: hosted by Luoyang Bureau of Cultural Relics and Luoyang Literature Federation, and organized by Luoyang Folk Museum and Luoyang Folk Artists Association. The aim of the fair is to present various intangible cultural heritage and unique craftsmanship in Heluo district, letting visitors from home and abroad experience Heluo culture. In order to fully demonstrate Heluo culture and use the folk fair as a strategy to protect and show Luoyang intangible cultural relics, this fair invited several representative local groups of Heluo district, including national intangible cultural relics project: Luoyang Xi Yang Hong Heluo Bass Drum Art Troupe, and Luoyang intangible cultural relics projects: Two Ghosts Wrestling, Royal Music of Empress Wu, puppet show by the Nanzhuang Puppet Troupe of Taoying, Ruyang county of Luoyang, etc.. It also held Luoyang Intangible Cultural Heritage Craftsmanship and Work of Arts Exhibition, inviting folk artists and intangible cultural heritage inheritors

俗博物馆也准备了一些民俗文化项目供游客观赏，如洛阳"太公"神鞭、偃师市天天乐宠物表演、罗山皮影、捏面人、小学生剪纸等。庙会期间，市民和游客还可以欣赏到面塑表演、剪纸艺术展示、卢氏木版年画展示、糖人捏塑表演等。

2010年第20届洛阳民俗文化庙会。这一届民俗文化庙会由洛阳市文物管理局和洛阳市文联主办，洛阳民俗博物馆和洛阳市民间艺术家协会承办。活动重点一是展示河洛地区丰富多彩的非物质文化遗产，二是进行洛阳地区民间工艺制作表演和展示活动，使中外游客领略河洛文化的魅力。为充分展示河洛地区的民俗文化，利用庙会平台，做好洛阳市非物质文化遗产的抢救、保护和展示工作，此届庙会邀请了一批河洛地区极具代表性的文艺团体和社火团队到庙会上进行表演。其中既有国家级非物质文化遗产项目洛阳市夕阳红河洛大鼓艺术团，又有洛阳市非物质文化遗产项目二鬼摔跤、武皇十万宫廷乐以及洛阳市汝阳县陶营乡南庄木偶剧团的木偶戏等。此届庙会还举办了"洛阳市非物质文化遗产传承技艺展演和民间艺术品展示活动"，邀请洛阳地区非物质文化遗产项目传承人和民间艺术家到庙会上表演和展示。另外，为丰富活动内容，此届庙会还举办了洛阳市名家书画作品展和洛阳市首届古今酒器展。其中，洛阳市名家书画作品展展出该市著名书画家沈丽洲、许素卿、许晓波、李新煌、李月娥5位名家书画作品100余幅，洛阳市首届古今酒器展展出洛阳市酒具收藏协会和该市文物管理局原局长马学增先生(已故)收藏的各类古今酒器300余件。为弘扬中国传统饮食文化，此届庙会还与中华民族美食巡展团合作，举办中华民族美食巡展活动，新疆羊肉串、开封灌汤包等几十种特色风味小吃使游客们在庙会

to perform on the scene for visitors. Furthermore, Calligraphy Works and Paintings of Famous Artists Exhibition and Luoyang First Ancient and Modern Drinking Vessels Exhibition were held during the fair to provide more activities for visitors. The Calligraphy Works and Paintings of Famous Artists Exhibition showed more than one hundred works from famous calligraphers and painters in Luoyang, such as Shen Lizhou, Xu Suqin, Xu Xiaobo, Li Xinhuang and Li Yue' e. Luoyang First Ancient and Modern Drinking Vessels Exhibition exhibited more than three hundred works collected by Luoyang Association of Drinking Vessels Collectors and Mr. Ma Xuezeng, former director of Luoyang Bureau of Cultural Relics. Besides, the folk fair held Chinese food fair with Chinese Food Troupe to promote traditional Chinese gastronomy, offering dozens of snacks, including Xinjiang mutton shish kebab and juicy steamed buns of Kaifeng for visitors to have a good time there.

The 22nd Luoyang folk fair in 2012: the folk fair in 2012 was hosted by Luoyang municipal government and organized by Luoyang Bureau of Cultural Relics. Its theme was to promote Heluo folk culture, demonstrate folk art, enrich peony cultural festival, and propel the development of tourism. The fair not only had various interesting folk art performances, such as Nanliu large drum performance, Ruyang selected scenes of drama, and Xingyang Jiang lion dance, but also national intangible cultural projects like Luoshan shadow show and Zhuxian wood engraving pictures exhibition. Besides, this fair specially held Outstanding Cultural Works of Arts Series Exhibitions: the 2012 Luoyang Outstanding Ancient and Modern Drinking Vessels Exhibition showed more than 1000 works including peony series, dragon series, historical characters series, Du Kang (a semi-legendary inventor of liquor in China) series, and mini vessels series. Wang Naixuan Works

上不仅逛得开心，而且吃得高兴。

2012年第22届洛阳民俗文化庙会。此届庙会由洛阳市政府主办，洛阳市文物管理局承办，主题是"弘扬河洛民间文化、展示民间艺术，烘托牡丹文化节喜庆气氛，服务旅游发展战略"。庙会上，不仅有异彩纷呈的民间文艺演出，如宜阳南留大型鼓乐表演、汝阳折子戏表演、荥阳蒋头狮舞表演等，还有国家级非物质文化遗产项目，如罗山皮影、朱仙镇木版年画等展演。此届庙会还特别设立了文化精品陈列展览。其中，"2012中国洛阳古今酒器精品展"共展出"牡丹酒器""龙型酒器""古今人物""杜康系列"和"微型酒器"等酒器1000余件。王耐萱丝绫堆绣（布贴）艺术展则展出了洛阳市非物质文化遗产项目——丝绫堆绣

（布贴）作品100余幅，题材包括戏曲人物、花卉、民间传说等。

of Siling Duixiu (cloth pasting painting) Exhibition exhibited more than one hundred works that used characters in drama, legends and flowers as themes.

（六）登山踏青

春天本来就是登山踏青的季节。洛阳的春天遍地都是牡丹花，边赏花边游玩，远离城市的喧嚣，来到野外呼吸新鲜空气，登高远眺，满目繁花，既锻炼身体，也能怡情，所以登山踏青也成了牡丹花会里的一项传统节日活动。不少市民和游客都喜欢选择登山踏青作为牡丹花节期间的主要活动之一。

在洛阳周边的乡镇里，村民们在田野山头都种植了不少牡丹花，虽然品种没有城里牡丹园的多，品相也不如城里牡丹园的好，但却能给人带来一种清新自然的田园风情。村民们说，每年牡丹花节来乡村里赏花的游客也不少，近几年来，村里还专门开设了农家乐、小客栈，并完善了交通等基础设施，以便更好地招待

Spring outings

Spring is the right time for mountain climbing and field trip. In spring, peony flowers are all over Luoyang. Visitors and citizens can appreciate peony flowers while having a spring outing, enjoying the tranquil countryside as well as breathing fresh air. This not only serves to improve their health, but also cultivates their taste. Therefore, it has been a traditional activity of peony festival since ancient times. In modern times, many visitors and citizens choose spring outing as one of their major activities during the peony festival.

In towns near Luoyang, farmers planted plenty of peonies in the field and mountains. Though these peony flowers are not precious and diverse as those in

the city, they look fresh and natural, forming part of the countryside scenery. Farmers in these towns say that there are many visitors coming here to appreciate peony every year. In recent years, many towns have built rural home inns and hotels, and improved the infrastructure to offer a better service for visitors. Take Wangcun Village of Cangtou Town, Xin'an County for example. Located in south of Xiaolangdi Reservoir, it is one of the most famous sites for peony appreciating in spring. The flowering period of peony there is around April 10th to April 30th when flowers bloom near rivers or over mountains, as lovely and elegant as fairies. In Wangcun, visitors not only appreciate peony, but also enjoy its beautiful landscape. The village is surrounded by waters on the north, east and west. Only its south is connected with other places by land. Wangcun started to plant peony three years ago and now its peony planting area reaches around 2000 *mu* (more than 133 hectares) with more than seventy species. Most visitors do self-drive tour there. They need to start from Luoyang, drive along Xiaolangdi express, and turn west when arriving Hanshui Village, Hengshui Town, Mengjin County till the gas station of Hengshui Village, Hengshui Town. After another 10 kilometers' drive to the northwest, they will reach the destination. Therefore, for visitors who have never been there before, it is really hard for them to find it without local guide. As most tree peonies are planted in mountains or on the slope, it was not convenient for visitors to have a closer look. Now Wangcun has built concrete road to the depths of peony gardens

外地来的赏花人。如新安县仓头镇王村，就是春季里适合踏青赏花的较有名的地点之一。该村的牡丹花盛开期在4月中下旬，在小浪底水库南侧，牡丹临泽而居，漫山遍野，远离尘嚣，如出尘仙子般清新脱俗。在这里，游人既可以观赏牡丹，也可以领略自然山水风光。该村地理位置特殊，三面临水，只有最南边与陆地相接。王村从3年前开始种牡丹，如今，该村的牡丹种植面积已有2000亩，囊括观赏牡丹中常见的70多个品种。来此的游客大多是自驾游，从洛阳市区出发，走小浪底专线，到达孟津县横水镇寒水村后向西行至横水镇横水村加油站，然后向西北方向行驶约10公里即可到达。对于头一次来的赏花客，如果没有当地老乡领路，这片栖身山野的牡丹还真不好找。由于牡丹大部分种在山坡上，游客要到近处观赏多了一些不便。不过，村里已修了水泥路，可延伸至牡丹园深处。现在，村里的农家饭店有四五家，游客可以品尝到野生鱼、野菜、土鸡等美味，人均消费约30元。

在现代洛阳牡丹花节里，登山除了作为一项民众休闲娱乐活动，也被发展成为一项有组织的体育竞技活动。不少景区都会举办登山节活动，制定登山路线和竞赛规则。每次登山活动都有不少游客自愿报名参加，比赛角逐非常激烈，参与者和旁观者都十分有激情，为节日增加了不少热烈的气氛。2012年第30届中国洛阳牡丹文化节的"天池山杯"登山公开赛受到了广泛关注，共有来自山东、湖北、重庆、河北、辽宁等地的近千人参加比赛。比赛起始点位于天池山景区入口，终点位于景区中心服务区，全程4.3公里。来自山东滨州的残疾小伙马明涛勇夺男子青年组冠军。夺冠后，他说："能来到繁花似锦的洛阳参加比赛，是我的荣幸，洛阳山清水秀、景色宜人，回到山东后，我会带动更多的家乡父老来洛阳参观旅游。"

and there are four to five restaurants offering fresh fish, local vegetables and chicken, with per capital consumption around 30 *yuan*.

In modern Luoyang peony festival, mountain climbing is both a popular recreational activity and an organized competitive sport. Many scenic spots hold mountain climbing competition, set route and rules, and have many visitors participating in the exciting match every year. The audience are also very passionate and have a great time. The Tian Chi Mountain Climbing Competition of the 30th peony festival in 2012 attracted great attention and had nearly one thousand participants from Shandong, Hubei, Hebei, Chongqing, Liaoning, etc. The start is the entrance of Tian Chi Mountain and the destination is the service area in the center, with whole distance reaching 4.3 kilometers. The championship was won by Ma Mingtao, a disabled young man from Bingzhou, Shandong. After winning, he said, "I am very honored to take part in this match. Luoyang has very pleasant scenery with clean water and high mountains. I will take my friends and families to come back here."

2.Modern activities

Performances and carnivals

Though performances and carnivals have existed since ancient times, they were never major events of peony festival. Due to the organization of host and the development of science and technology, performances and carnivals become the major activities of modern peony festival. Performances of previous peony festivals include indoor and outdoor shows, traditional singings, dances, dramas, folk art performances, and modern popular arts like hip-hop and ballroom dance.

Performances of the 29th Peony Festival in 2011: the opening ceremony gala of the 29th Peony Cultural Festival was held in the stadium of Luoyang new district. Gathering many famous stars home and abroad, it gave audience a wonderful experience. The gala consisted of four parts: national beauty and celestial fragrance, charm of ancient capital, capital of peony, and prosperous China. 80% of its songs and dances were specially made for Luoyang peony culture and the ancient city. By using multi-media

二、现代型活动

（一）文艺表演、狂欢活动

其实文艺表演、狂欢活动古已有之，但并不是洛阳牡丹花会的主体活动。由于现代科学技术的发展和有主办方进行集中策划与安排，文艺表演与狂欢活动成了现代洛阳牡丹文化节的主要活动之一。在历届牡丹文化节的文艺会演中，既有室内晚会，也有露天表演，既有舞台剧的表演，也有民间文艺串烧，既有传统歌舞，也有现代流行文艺如街舞、国标舞等元素的加入。

2011年第29届洛阳牡丹文化节期间，于洛阳市新区体育场举办的洛阳牡丹文化节开幕式文艺晚会齐集众多国内外明星，为观众带来一场大型多媒体视听盛宴。晚会共分为四大篇章——国色天香、古都神韵、牡丹花城、盛世腾飞，80%的歌词和舞蹈是为洛阳牡丹文化和千年帝都文化量身打造的。

在舞台设计上运用了多媒体技术，将整体舞台的美术造型投射成一朵高20米、宽140米、深80米的巨大牡丹花，表演者可在其中展现时隐时现的神奇景象。著名影视演员陈数和中央电视台主持人任鲁豫担任晚会主持人，毛阿敏、杨洪基、佟铁鑫、戴玉强、萨顶顶、潘玮柏、凤凰传奇组合、旭日阳刚组合等声乐演员带来了一首首带有牡丹特色文化的歌曲，著名豫剧大师马金凤演唱了经典豫剧曲目《穆桂英挂帅》，沈阳军区前进杂技团为观众带来了惊险刺激的杂技表演……除国内一流明星之外，来自蒙古的迪给、非洲的玛利亚和郝歌也在开幕式晚会上献艺。

而于4月1日至30日在周王城广场举行的"河洛欢歌·广场文化狂欢月"活动，每天都有一场精彩、炫目的专业文艺演出，观众如果自己看不过瘾，还可走上"百姓舞台"，一露身手，

technology, the whole stage was made like a twenty-meter high, one hundred and forty meters wide, and eighty meters deep peony flower, with performers standing in the heart of it. The hosts were Chen Shu, one famous movie star and Ren Luyu, a M.C. of CCTV. Many famous singers including Mao Aming, Yang Hongji, Tong Tiexin, Dai Yuqiang, Sa Dingding, Pan Weibo, Fenghuang Chuanqi (Phenix Legend) and Xuri Yanggang(Masculine Sunrise) sang songs for peony and peony culture. Ma Jinfeng, a master of Henan opera, performed classical scene "Lady General Mu Takes Command" and Qianjin Acrobatic Troupe from Shenyang military region gave an exciting and thrilling performance for the audience. Besides Chinese stars, artists of Mongolia and Africa also performed in the gala.

Happily Singing in Heluo and Culture Carnivals were held in Wangcheng Square every day from April 1st to April 30th. Citizens and visitors not only could watch professional and exciting shows, but also go to People's Stage to show their talents if not satisfied with merely watching. During the month of cultural carnivals, one thousand people took peony body building exercises with the sound of row drums and disk drums which can be heard thousand miles away. The peony magic show performed by more than one hundred students was also a sight feast for audience there. During April 3rd to April 29th, from 3:30 p.m. to 5 p.m every day, there were also special shows with wonderful and various performances from different counties, college students and even teenagers. Audience there enjoyed the amazing performance and performers happily showed their talents and courage.People's Stage performances began from 5 p.m to 5:30 p.m during April 3rd to April 29th. Any citizens or visitors who are good at singing, dancing, drama, opera, or acrobatics could go there to perform as long as they want. To guarantee that citizens and visitors can watch performances near their home or hotels, Happily Singing in Heluo and Culture Carnivals had 6 sub-stages in old district, Xigong district, Jianxi district, Luolong district, Chanhe Hui district and Jili district. From April 2rd to April 30th, many unique performances were shown in these stages.

台上台下一起狂欢。在狂欢活动中，洛阳本地的排鼓和盘鼓相继敲响，鼓声铿锵有力，响彻云霄。阵容庞大、场面壮观的千人牡丹健身舞也随之起舞。此外，百余位学生表演的"魔术牡丹群舞"也给人们带来魔幻无穷的视觉享受。在4月3日至4月29日每天15时30分至17时进行的专场文艺演出中，节目形式和内容多种多样，有来自各县（市）区的专场演出，也有大中专院校的精彩节目，更有青少年一展才艺。站在台下看节目是一种享受，而走上舞台展示自我则是一种勇气。4月3日至4月29日每天17时至17时30分，"百姓舞台"开演，有声乐、舞蹈、戏剧、曲艺、杂技等绝活的市民和游客均可走上舞台，有才就可"秀"出来。为了方便市民和游客就近观看节目，"河洛欢歌·广场文化狂欢月"设有老城区、西工区、涧西区、洛龙区、瀍河回族区、吉利区6个分会场，从4月2日起一直持续到4

月30日，在不同的分会场都能欣赏到独具特色的文艺节目。

2011年是牡丹花会升格为国家级节会的第一年，该年活动在阵容和规模上较往年有了很大提高，市民和游客可以欣赏到来自中央、省级歌舞院团的著名艺术家和知名演员的精彩表演。曲艺表演艺术家范军、庆波带来了相声《开心十分》、豫剧表演艺术家王惠表演了豫剧《五世请缨选段》、北京军区战友文工团的歌唱家陈真带来了歌伴舞《中国牡丹》、洛阳群众艺术馆青年歌唱家姬丽娜演唱了歌曲《盛开的牡丹》等。

从4月4日至5月7日的这一个多月的时间里，"中华人民共和国文化部首届优秀保留剧目大奖获奖剧目·洛阳展演月"也在洛阳歌剧院演出了8部精品剧目。这8部精品剧目均为国家文化部首届优秀保留剧目大奖获

2011 was the first year when peony festival became a national event, and its performances and carnival activities were further enlarged and improved. Audience could enjoy excellent programmes from artists of central and provincial opera and dance troupes, such as cross talk Very Happy performed by Fan Jun and Qing Bo, Henan drama Twelve Widows' West Expedition performed by Wang Hui, a well-known artist, Peony of China performed by Chen Zhen, a singer with art troupe of Beijing military region, and Blooming Peony performed by Ji Lina, a young singer of Luoyang Mass Arts Center.

From April 4th to May 7th, eight excellent repertoires chosen by the Ministry of Culture from The First Outstanding Repertoire Award were shown in Luoyang Theater, including modern drama, dance drama, Beijing opera, Shaoxing opera, Sichuan opera, child play and puppet show. It was their first time to be shown in Luoyang. In the modern drama *Father*, Song Guofeng, national class-A actor and winner of many national rewards, presented audience a torturous but warm story of a old model worker's family in the northeast of China in the late 1990s. *Silk Road and Flower Rain*, a dance drama praised as "as if made in heaven with people on earth having few times to watch", used well-known Dunhuang frescoes and silk road as the subject, with expressive dance and unique style, to depict a moving story of how painter Zhang, his daughter Yingniang and a Persia businessman bore hardships together and made lifelong friends. *Malan Flower*, created when China Children's Art Theatre was established and being its best drama, was successfully transferred to a fairy musical play in 1990. Its mythical music, fluent plot, and exciting dances gave audience a wonderful experience. Other dramas included *Celebrating Mother's Birthday* by Zhejiang Xiaobaihua Shaoxing Opera Troupe, *Flaming Mountains* by Quanzhou Puppet Troupe of Fujian, *Dreams of Dunhuang*, a folk dance drama

奖剧目，有话剧、舞剧、京剧、越剧、川剧及儿童剧、木偶剧，都是首次来洛阳演出。其中，国家一级演员、获得过多个国家级奖项的著名话剧演员宋国锋，在话剧《父亲》中，为观众讲述了发生在20世纪90年代中后期的东北工业老城，在一个老劳模、老工人家中发生的非常曲折但又不失温情的故事。被誉为"此舞只应天上有，人间难得看几回"的舞剧《丝路花雨》，是以举世闻名的敦煌壁画和丝绸之路为题材，用富有表现力的舞姿和别具一格的艺术风格，为观众描绘了敦煌画工神笔张和其女儿英娘与波斯商人患难与共、生死相交的动人故事。中国儿童艺术剧院的建院剧目、"镇院之作"——儿童剧《马兰花》，于1990年成功向童话音乐剧转型，剧中神秘的音乐、流畅的剧情、热闹的群舞为全剧增添了浪漫气氛。另外还有浙江小百花越剧团带来的越剧《五女拜寿》、福建泉州

市木偶剧团带来的木偶剧《火焰山》、兰州大剧院的大型原创民族舞剧《大梦敦煌》、北京京剧院的京剧《三打陶三春》以及重庆市川剧院的川剧《金子》。

（二）竞技比赛

竞技比赛能为节日增添热烈气氛，提高群众的参与度与积极性，普及全民健身的体育精神。除了前文所介绍的登山比赛，在洛阳牡丹花节里还举办了国标舞大赛、健美操赛、鞭陀公开赛、摩托车拉力赛、攀岩大赛、拉练赛、武术比赛等竞技活动。

2012年洛阳牡丹文化节上，为纪念玄奘诞辰1412周年，第七届"玄奘之路"中欧戈壁挑战赛偃师拉练赛在偃师市举行，来自中欧国际工商学院的五十多名选手参加徒步跋涉大赛。中欧国际工商学院坚持每年举办"玄奘之路"国际商学院戈壁挑战赛选拔赛，得到了国内外

by Lanzhou Theatre, *Three Fights with Tao* from Beijing Opera Theatre and *Gold* by Chongqing Sichuan Opera Theatre.

Competitive matches

Competitive matches can make festivals more exciting, enhance mass participation, and improve people's health. Besides previously mentioned mountain-climbing, Luoyang Peony Festival also holds ballroom dancing competition, aerobics contest, spinning-top open, motorcycle rally, rock-climbing match, long distance hike, and martial arts tournament.

During the 2012 Luoyang Peony Festival, Yanshi Marathon of the Seventh Road of Xuanzang China Europe Gobi Challenge was held in Yanshi to celebrate the 1412th anniversary of Monk Xuanzang's birthday. More than fifty participants from China Europe International Business School attended in the match. Held by China Europe International Business School every year, the competition drew nationwide attention and was of significant importance to promote Yanshi and the spirit of Xuanzang. As the hometown of Xuanzang, Yanshi worked hard to establish its fame and promote Xuanzang's spirit. The whole journey was forty-five kilometers long, starting from Hakka People Emigrating South Memorial Square of Hutou Moutain, to the crossing between North Perimeter Rd and Phoenix Rd, then heading west to Xinggou Village, Shouyangshan Town, climbing over Mangshan Mountain to reach the old watercourse of Yellow River, and finally Shouyang Mountain Forest Park. The whole route included flat road, narrow footpath between fields, unsurfaced road, and river bank, bringing a lot of challenges to participants. They had to overcome all the difficulties and tried their best to finish the match.

Luoyang is also called the capital of ballroom dance. More than twenty thousand people in Luoyang are learning ballroom dance and it has held many national ballroom dance competitions to promote fitness activities and enhance people's health awareness. The 13th National Ballroom Dance Competition in Tourist Cities in 2011 attracted more than two thousand dancers and honored guests from home and abroad. The organizing committee

的高度关注，反响强烈，对宣传偃师、弘扬玄奘精神具有重要意义。偃师市作为玄奘大师的家乡，着力打造玄奘故里的文化名片。该活动是一场体验式文化赛事，选拔赛分为男、女个人徒步计时赛。比赛起点为虎头山客家人南迁纪念广场下，北环路与凤凰大道交叉口，西至首阳山镇刑沟村，然后向北，翻过邙山，到达黄河故道，回经首阳山森林公园，全程45公里。比赛途中，既有平坦的公路，又有田间小道、河堤土路，给参赛队员带来不小挑战。参赛队员必须克服困难，挑战自我，超越极限才能完成这场拉练赛。

洛阳又被称为"国标舞之都"，全市有超过两万人在学习国标舞。结合这一情况，洛阳牡丹文化节已举办多届全国性的国标舞大赛，借此推动全民健身活动的深入开展，提高人民群众的健身意识。2011年第13届全国旅游城市国标舞大赛上，国内外

2000多位专业选手及嘉宾齐聚洛阳，举行千人共跳国标舞活动。大赛特邀请连续11年担任全国国标舞锦标赛评审专家的李虹做现场指导，由国标舞蹈家联合会国际级考官、来自俄罗斯和亚美尼亚等国的20多位知名专业评审执裁。活动设立职业组、专业院校组、成人组、少儿组等多个组别，本着"以舞会友、重在参与、公平、公正、公开"的原则进行，为国内外爱好舞蹈的朋友架起了一座相互学习、合作、交流的桥梁。

（三）新型文化活动

洛阳牡丹文化节除了牡丹诗会、书画展等传统节日活动，还有一些现代新型文化活动，如学术研讨会、摄影展以及各种特色主题展览等。

学术研讨会

洛阳牡丹文化节是一个具有深厚文化内涵的民俗节日，一直受到国内

invited Li Hong, who had been the judge of national ballroom dance competitions for eleven years, to be on-the-spot guide. They also invited more than twenty experts in this field from China, Russia, Armenia, and Ballroom Dancers Federation to be the judges. During the competition, One-thousand People Dance was held. The competition consisted of four categories: professionals, students from specialized institutions, amateur adults and amateur teenagers. Based on the principle of "meeting friends through dance; participation matters more than results; fair, open and impartial", it served as a bridge for Chinese and foreign dance lovers to cooperate, exchange ideas and learn from each other.

New cultural activities

Besides traditional festival activities like poetry reading, calligraphy works and painting exhibitions, Luoyang Peony Cultural Festival also holds new cultural activities, such as symposiums, photo shows, and exhibitions of various themes.

Symposiums

As a folk festival with rich culture, Luoyang peony cultural festival has drawn much international attention. Many academic sectors conducted related studies on it. Holding related symposiums during the festival and exchanging ideas can make great contribution to the regional development. Luoyang has held many symposiums on peony and Luoyang during the peony festival, such as Tourism Development Forum in the 28th Luoyang Peony Festival, Luoyang World Cultural Heritage Protection and Utilization Forum in the 29th Peony Festival and China Cultural Industry Summit in the 30th Luoyang Peony Festival. On the forum of Forbes China Central Region's Self-employment and Private Sector Development in the 30th Luoyang Peony Festival, many influential experts shared their opinions and gave keynote speeches, tackling issues like the transition of central region's economic structure. They also discussed the rise of central China and how Chinese enterprises become World Top 500 during the Round Table Dialogue section. Some Forbes invited guests and famous managers even talked to local outstanding managers one to one on the investment and enterprise development.

外学界的高度重视，许多学科和专业都对该节日有相关研究。在节日中召开各类学术研讨会，可促进相关研究的交流与总结，从而对地区发展与进步作出贡献。如第28届洛阳牡丹文化节举办的休闲旅游产业发展论坛、第29届洛阳牡丹文化节举办的2011世界文化遗产保护与利用（洛阳）高峰论坛、第30届洛阳牡丹文化节举办的中国文化产业专业高峰论坛等。在第30届洛阳牡丹文化节期间举办的福布斯中国中原经济区自主创业与民营经济发展论坛上，多位在此专业领域内有影响力的嘉宾进行了主题演讲，演讲内容包括中原经济结构该如何转型等；在深度圆桌对话上不少嘉宾就"关于中部崛起的宏观思考"、"逐鹿中原，全球500强的新机会"等问题进行了对话；福布斯特邀嘉宾、知名企业负责人与洛阳优秀国企、高增长企业就投资与发展展开了一对一的座谈。

摄影展

每年牡丹花会期间，不少摄影爱好者都会用手机和相机代替传统的绘画来记录下牡丹的每一个美丽的瞬间，含苞时的青涩，绽放时的绚烂，凋零时的坚强，晴天的光彩照人，雨天的清新脱俗，都被摄影家们一一记录。虽然牡丹盛开有时，生命有限，但一旦被拍摄进人们的镜头里，就能变成永恒的美丽。

其他各类特色主题展览

在洛阳牡丹文化节上，还有一些结合了地区文化特色与时代气息的文化活动。2012年第30届洛阳牡丹文化节上，为响应洛阳市发展文化产业、打造动漫之都的号召，举办了首届动漫节。12个社团为市民和游客奉献了一场精彩的动漫盛宴，带来了《仙剑奇侠传》《最终幻想》等13个精彩节目，世界COSPLAY峰会银奖得主"地狱蝴蝶丸"专程从香港赶来，与动漫爱好者

Photo shows

During the peony festival, many photographers use their cameras or mobile phones, instead of brushes and pens to record every beautiful moment of peony flowers: their first bloom, full blossom, withering, shining appearance under sunshine, and lovely look in the rain. All these are recorded by photographers. Though the flowering period of peony is limited, once their beauty is captured in the camera, it becomes eternal.

Other exhibitions

Luoyang peony festival also holds many cultural activities that combined local features and modern elements. During the 30th Luoyang Peony Festival, the first comic-con was held to boost cultural industry and develop Luoyang as the capital of cartoon. Twelve troupes nationwide provided thirteen performances, including cosplay of The Legend of Swordsman and Fairy, and Final Fantasy. Diyu Hudie Wan (Butterfly Momoko in Hell), the silver award winner of world COSPLAY summit, came to Luoyang from Hong Kong and gave a wonderful show with other cartoon lovers. Their refined dress and devoted performance attracted many visitors.

During the festival, Luoyang Museum held two exhibitions showing the characteristics of local cultures: The Soul of Grand Canal, and Silk Road and Luoyang, exhibiting one hundred and twenty pictures of excavated Grand Canal, photos of the relics, and more than one hundred and fifty antiques of silk road. Some of the valuable antiques had never been shown in public. The Pivot of Grand Canal: Grand Canal and Luoyang Exhibition consisted of six parts: canal building, canal utilization, the pivot: Luoyang, changes of canal, canal management, and its application for world heritage. The exhibition systematically demonstrated the development and changes of Grand Canal, showing Luoyang's important status and role in its development. The Start of Silk Road: Silk Road and Luoyang consisted of five parts: the origin of Silk Road, its establishment, its development, its heyday, and application for world heritage of Luoyang part, presenting the importance of Luoyang in the history of Silk Road. The antiques shown on the exhibitions included gold and silver ware, china, tri-coloured glazed potteries of the Tang Dynasty, colored potteries, stone ware and glass ware. It was the first time for Luoyang to hold exhibitions on Silk Road comprehensively. Visitors could also see other exhibitions like Heluo Civilization, Potteries of the Han and Tang Dynasties, Tri-coloured

同台献艺。现场观众们被演员精致的装扮和投入的表演所吸引。

在此届牡丹花节上，洛阳市博物馆还展出了两场结合地区文化的特色主题展览：“运河之魂”展览与“丝绸之路与洛阳”展览，共展出120张大运河考古发现图片、现存遗迹图片以及150余件（组）丝绸之路文物，其中部分珍贵展品是首次与大众见面。“运河中枢——大运河与洛阳”展览，包括大运河的先声、大运河的开通、大运河的中枢——洛阳、大运河的变迁、大运河的管理和大运河申遗等六大部分，全面系统地展示了大运河的形成、发展、变迁历程，讲述了洛阳在大运河发展史上的地位和作用。“丝路起点——丝绸之路与洛阳”展览，包括丝绸之路的萌芽、丝绸之路的确立、丝绸之路的发展、丝绸之路的鼎盛和丝绸之路洛阳段申遗等五大部分，再现了洛阳在丝绸之路发展史上的重要地位，其中精选的珍贵文物涵盖金银器、瓷器、唐三彩、彩绘陶器、石器、玻璃器等，这是洛阳市首次全面系统地举办丝绸之路文物展。另外，人们还可在博物馆中欣赏河洛文明展、汉唐陶俑展、唐三彩展、石刻艺术展及宫廷珍宝展等六大专题展览。

（四）其他活动

经济活动

牡丹节中的经济活动有投资贸易洽谈会、城市投资与发展论坛、旅游商品交易会、车展、美食节等，不仅使节日活动更加多元化，也展示了洛阳的经济发展水平，促进了区域发展。以车展为例。车展是每年牡丹花节上较受人关注的活动之一，尤其是受到年轻人和汽车摄影爱好者的喜欢。而节日中的车展更是与其他时期、其他地区的车展有所不同，将名车展示与牡丹元素、洛阳景相结合，是洛

Glazed Potteries of the Tang Dynasty, Stone Carvings Exhibition, and Royal Antiques Exhibition.

Other activities

Economic activities

Economic activities held during the peony festival include investment and trade fair, city development and investment forum, trade fair of tourist commodities, auto show, food festival, etc.. They make festival activities more diverse, show the economic strength of Luoyang, and promote regional development. Take auto show for example, it is one of the most eye-catching activities during the festival and is especially popular among young people and auto photographers. Different from auto shows in other places, Luoyang auto show combines the elements of Luoyang, peony, and car show together. For instance, the 11th auto show held in 2012 built a several-kilometer-long scenic gallery by taking advantage of Luoyang's characteristics, site condition, and the experience of other national auto shows. Themed as auto, it was added with the element of peony and was fully functional. Every section of the gallery was assigned to different functions and had special design, forming beautiful scenery there.

Exchanges with other places

Thanks to the development of IT, transportation and other industries, the exchanges among different places have been strengthened and limitations on locations become fewer and fewer. Not only visitors and activities from other places can enter Luoyang, activities of peony festival can also be held in other places during the peony festival.

On March 7th, 2010, six hundred tree peonies of more than twenty species were taken by Luoyang delegation to participate the 2010 Taipei International Flora Expo, competing with other flowers worldwide and showing the elegance and beauty of the king of flowers. The expo especially arranged a 170-square-meter district: The Spring

阳牡丹节上车展的特色。如2012年第11届名车展，在充分吸纳国内顶级车展布展经验的基础上，车展结合洛阳城市特色和场地条件，按照"汽车主题、牡丹元素、景观长廊、功能完善"的要求，对展区进行功能规划及形象包装，在车展期间形成延绵数公里的汽车景观长廊。

两地交流活动

现代信息、交通、运输等行业的发展，加强了区域之间的交流与联系，也使得节日的地区限制越来越小，不仅外地的游客与活动能进入洛阳，同时，洛阳牡丹花节的相关节日活动也能同步在其他地区举办。

2010年3月7日，洛阳牡丹花首批20多个品种，共600株，随洛阳市赴台参展团启程前往宝岛台湾参加2010台北国际花卉博览会，与世界各地的名贵花卉共同争艳台北，彰显花中之王清香四溢的华贵尊容。台北国际花卉博览会"争艳馆"专门为洛阳牡丹开辟了170余平方米的"洛阳春天"展区，专门展出这批名贵的牡丹，使台湾同胞和世界各地游人在台北就能一睹高雅端庄、国色天香的牡丹风采。除牡丹花外，还有10个牡丹插花作品、100幅牡丹摄影作品、100幅牡丹字画和一批洛阳相关的文化艺术品等一同在这次博览会上亮相。

2010年7月，孟津县的平乐牡丹画作为河南活动周节目之一在上海世博会上尽显光彩，受到中外游客称奇和赞叹。在世博园宝钢大舞台非物质文化遗产传习区，来自平乐村的农民画家们，用一双双粗糙的手，绘出一幅幅国色天香、娇艳富贵的牡丹画，让无数参观者惊叹不已。为了向外国游客推介牡丹和农民牡丹画，农民画师郭泰森来上海之前，还专门印刷了宣传单页，在每段中文的后面附上英文介绍。每个在他展位前

of Luoyang in Pavilion of Dreams, for people from Taiwan and other places to appreciate the elegant and fragrant flowers. Besides peony flowers, ten peony arrangement works, one hundred peony photos, one hundred peony paintings and calligraphy works, and many works of arts on Luoyang were shown on the expo.

In July 2010, Mengjin Pingle peony painting show, as a program during the Henan week of the Shanghai Expo, attracted a lot of visitors from home and abroad. Farmer painters were arranged in the Intangible World Heritage Teaching and Learning Center on Bao Steel Stage. Their gorgeous and elegant peony flowers, painted by the hands which were used to do farm work, amazed many visitors. To introduce peony and farmers' peony paintings, Guo Taiseng , one of the farmer painters, made several hand-outs in both Chinese and English and printed "Luoyang peony is the best in China" on his stand so that every visitor passing by could see it. Guo felt quite happy for being able to promote peony to the world through this stage. On July 15th, under the invitation of Changning District Government of Shanghai, five Pingle farmer painters went to Xinhua Road to paint on sight and gave their paintings to citizens there, receiving warm welcome and high praise. This activity also promoted the cultural exchanges between Henan and Shanghai. On that day in the afternoon, some of the farmer painters went to Shanghai Second Armed Police Detachment to extend their regards to policemen from Henan. They talked with the policemen and painted peony pictures for them, offering spiritual comfort and got big welcome.

In 2011, Luoyang peony festival gained two venues in Beijing and Shanghai. The venue in Beijing was Liulihe Tianxiang Peony Garden with four major events held: Luoyang Peony Show, Luoyang Scenic Spots Exhibition, Peony Stamps Show, and Ode to Peony Dance, comprehensively presenting Luoyang peony culture. As the sole specialized peony planting garden in Beijing, Liulihe Tianxiang Peony Garden was around

停留的游客，几乎都会下意识地说一声：洛阳牡丹甲天下。能在这个世界舞台上，为宣传洛阳牡丹出力，让牡丹走向世界，他感到特别满足。7月15日，应上海市长宁区政府的邀请，平乐牡丹画农民画家一行5人，到长宁区新华街道为社区居民现场作画、赠画，受到了长宁区政府和广大市民的一致好评和赞赏，增进了河南与上海的文化合作交流。当天下午，平乐农民画家又走进上海武警二支队慰问在沪服役的河南籍战士，与战士们交流，为战士们现场作画、赠画，给子弟兵送去精神食粮，受到了广大官兵的热烈欢迎。

2011年，洛阳牡丹文化节首次在北京与上海举办分会场活动。北京分会场活动在琉璃河天香牡丹园举办，组织安排了"洛阳牡丹观赏""洛阳旅游风光""牡丹邮票展销"以及大型歌舞"牡丹颂"等几大主题活动，集中展现了洛阳的牡丹特色文化。北京琉璃河天香牡丹园占地110亩，共种植牡丹160多个品种，4万余株，园内设有牡丹仙子雕像、牡丹亭、洛阳旅游风光展等，是北京地区唯一的专业牡丹种植园区。由于天气原因，洛阳牡丹在4月20日左右会陆续开放，花期为15天左右。北京分会场活动的举办，使得北京市民不出北京便可观赏洛阳牡丹，领略洛阳风光。活动开幕当天，就有数千名北京市民前往天香牡丹园赏花。上海分会场活动在上海植物园举行，共设置了"国色天香""浪漫春色""花之海洋""精品荟萃"4个牡丹主题展区，"国色天香"展区有9个牡丹主题景点，俨然一个牡丹特色文化园；"浪漫春色"展区共展出了160多个品种2万多株牡丹；"花之海洋"展区有一处圆形花坛，花坛内有一处名为"源·园·缘"的牡丹主题景点；"精品荟萃"牡丹文化展区展出20余幅牡丹古画、22件牡丹插花艺术作品、约100幅与牡丹有关的当代名人字画以及牡丹瓷、

110 *mu* (more than seven hectares) and had more than forty thousand tree peonies of more than one hundred and sixty species. It also included the statue of peony fairy, peony pavilion, Luoyang scenic spots exhibition, etc.. Due to the influence of weather there, peony flowers began to bloom around April 20th and lasted half a month, enabling Beijing citizens to appreciate Luoyang peony and learn more about Luoyang without leaving Beijing. The first day when the event started, several thousand Beijing citizens went there to admire peony flowers' beauty. The venue in Shanghai was Shanghai Botanical Garden. There were four theme exhibitions: National Beauty and Celestial Fragrance, Romantic Spring, Sea of Flowers and Outstanding Peony Works Exhibition. The National Beauty and Celestial Fragrance Exhibition had nine theme scenic spots, looking like a peony garden. Romantic Spring section had more than twenty thousand tree peonies of more than one hundred and sixty species. The Sea of Flowers had a round flower bed with a theme spot named Source, Garden, and Lucky-chance (the three words have the same pronunciation of *yuan* in Chinese) and Outstanding Peony Works Exhibition showed more than twenty ancient peony paintings, twenty-two peony arrangement works, and around one hundred peony calligraphy works and paintings. Many peony works of arts like china, peony food like pancakes,

and peony philatelic products including postcards, stamps, commemorative envelopes and postmarks were also exhibited there. Now a new venue has been established in Chongqing.

牡丹饼等与牡丹有关的工艺品和农副产品，还有明信片、邮票、纪念封、邮戳等牡丹主题邮品。目前，洛阳牡丹文化节分会场活动已延伸到北京、上海与重庆。

Blind date activity

交友活动

As blind date becomes more and more popular in China, Luoyang peony festival held Blooming Peony Flowers Bring Happy Blind Date. Ten thousand people participated in it and made the festival more romantic. Organizers built some booths for single men and women to exchange their information and there were many staff and volunteers from all sectors helping to arrange date for single people. It is said that this activity helped many people get married.

随着现代交友活动的日益盛行，牡丹花节上也办起了以牡丹传情的"万人公益交友会"，为节日增添了一丝浪漫气息。活动制定了征婚板块，为前来参加交友相亲的单身男女提供交友资料，活动现场还有工作人员及社会各界的热心人士自愿组成"义务红娘"志愿者服务队，为前来征婚的人士安排约会。通过这一活动，不少单身男女组建了家庭。

3 节日带来的影响
Influence of Luoyang Peony Festival

经过30余年的发展，洛阳牡丹花会已由创办之初的赏花节会变成一个融赏花观灯、旅游观光、经贸合作与交流为一体的大型综合性经济文化活动，从地方节日发展成为一个国内外共同关注的国家级节日。节日的发展，给当地的群众生活、地区文化、区域发展等都产生了很大的影响，节日已融入洛阳社会的方方面面。

一、给人们带来休闲娱乐与快乐

休闲娱乐应该算是民俗节日，尤其是现代旅游节日的最基础的作用之一。

After thirty years' development, Luoyang peony festival has been developed from a city-level fair to a national festival with international influence, from a merely peony appreciating activity to a comprehensive event combining peony appreciating, lantern show, traveling, economic cooperation and exchanges together. Its growth has brought great influence and changes to local people's life, Luoyang culture and regional development. Now the festival is integrated into every aspect of Luoyang.

1. Provide more entertainment and happiness for people

Recreation is one of the basic functions of folk festivals and modern tourism festivals. As the pace of life in modern times, especially in cities, is very fast and people have to bear a lot of stress from work and life, festivals can serve to slow down the life pace and make people relaxed. With Luoyang peony festival's activities covering many areas such as sports, entertainment and games, citizens and visitors there not only admire wonderful shows, but also participate in activities to have a great time. During the festival, many people, whether having a spring outing with families or getting together with friends in three or five, put their work aside, totally relax themselves and enjoy the happy festival.

Travel notes of Luoyang peony festival: relax and enjoy the beauty

Luoyang peony festival brings the joy of leisure and beauty to visitors, which is demostrated in the following travel notes.

Travel note 1[①]: With my admiration for ancient capital, I came to Luoyang in warm spring breeze.

现代社会生活，尤其是城市社会生活，总是节奏快压力大。而节日的举办，能调节日常生活中繁忙紧张的生活节奏，使人放松心情。洛阳牡丹花会的节日活动丰富多彩，涉及文娱体育等各个方面，既有观赏性的表演展览，也有参与式的游戏比赛，能给市民和游客带来轻松与欢笑。在节日期间，很多市民与游客，或者全家人一起出门踏青，或者相约三五好友聚会游玩，大家都暂时将工作的事情抛在脑后，彻底地放松自己，沉浸于节日的欢乐气氛。

（一）节日给游客带来休闲与美的享受

洛阳牡丹节给游客带来了休闲与美的享受，从下面的游记中可见一斑。

游记1[①]：心中怀着对千年帝都的几分仰慕，

①Selected from: http://www.ilvping.com/travels/linetip-id-8041.html.

①节选自：http://www.ilvping.com/travels/linetip-id-8041.html。

在暖暖春风中，我来到了洛阳。洛阳给人的第一感觉还不错，沿纱厂路向南走，飞雕彩绘的楼宇、干净而充满绿意的街道，看起来很美丽，有序。汽车行至中州路，几排高楼又给古都增加了几分现代气息，路北是一派中国古代建筑，与路南的西方建筑相映生辉，路面破旧了一点，但绿草如茵，古代文明和现代文明交相辉映，自然与文化和谐交融，顿时颇觉不虚此行。王城公园的牡丹比我想象的少了一点，不过到底是国色天香，此言不虚。牡丹仙子雍容端庄，很圣洁的形象。人多了一点，还有很多国际友人。中午在牡丹城宾馆休息，服务生很热情，在12层楼上看洛阳市容，满目翠绿，绿化得很不错。打车去龙门，和洛阳的哥谈得很开心。我惊奇地发现洛阳除了人文景观，还有那么多自然景观，花果山竟然是洛阳的！还有龙峪湾、小浪底、鸡冠洞……沿途到了关林，这是一个古代经典

My first impression on Luoyang is quite good. When driving south along Shachang Road, I saw green trees, clean streets and buildings with carvings and colorful paintings. All looked beautiful and ordered. The famous Zhongzhou Road has several high buildings which add Luoyang with some modern elements. Its north are traditional Chinese buildings and its south are western buildings, enhancing both sides' beauty. Though the road was a little old and shabby, green grass on its sides decorated it well. I thus sensed a harmonious existence of ancient and modern civilization and felt this journey was not fruitless. When I reached Wangcheng Park, the peony flowers were not as much as I had expected, but they indeed had the national beauty and celestial fragrance. The statue of peony fairy looked elegant and noble. Many people were appreciating peony there, some of whom even came from foreign countries. In the noon, I had some rest in Mudan Cheng Hotel (the city of peony) and enjoyed a good service. As my room was on the twelfth floor, I got a panoramic view of Luoyang and found trees planted all over the city. In the afternoon, I took a taxi to Longmen Grottoes and had a good chat with the taxi driver. I surprisingly learned that besides cultural relics, there were many national scenic spots in Luoyang. The Mountain of Flowers and Fruits (the birthplace of Monkey King in *Journey to the West*) is in Luoyang. Luoyang also has Long Yu Valley, Xiaolangdi Reservoir, Jiguan Limestone Cave, etc.. We passed Guan Lin Temple on the way, which was a classic ancient architecture. When I arrived at Longmen Grottoes and saw the statue of Grand Vairocana Buddha, I was totally shocked by its sublime and was full of respect for it. Though I was never a Buddhism believer, I closed my palms like a monk with piety...

Travel Note 2[1]: To escape noisy city and experience another life during the Tomb-Sweeping Festival, I went to ancient capital Xi'an and Luoyang. It happened that Luoyang peony festival was being held when I arrived there. Seeing the gorgeous flowers, I was full of joys. In the evening, I went to visit peony lantern show. The peony flowers looked quite charming under colorful lights. Some of them just began to bloom, and some had been in full blossom, making people feel the beauty of nature. Whenever I recalled the seven-day journey, people I met and things I saw would appear clearly in my mind like a movie. Whether happy and exciting moments, or unsatisfying incidents, they all are the most valuable souvenirs for me.

Thoughts of a peony festival participant: enjoy the process

Luoyang peony festival also offers the joy to

建筑群。到了龙门石窟，当看到卢舍那大佛时，我深深地被震撼了！如此壮观如此无言，心中的崇敬无法形容，从不信佛的我虔诚地合起了手掌……

游记2[1]：躲开城市的喧嚣，趁着清明节，穿越时空，近距离接触十三朝古都西安，九朝古都洛阳……正值洛阳牡丹花会，一片热闹景象，心花怒放。夜游牡丹灯会，国花牡丹在强灯光的照耀下，格外迷人，有的含苞待放，有的绽放光芒，让人感受到了自然之美。七天的访古之旅很快就结束了，每每回忆时，就像放电影，不同人、事、物的片段清晰地在脑海中出现。无论经历的是欢乐、惊险，抑或是愤怒、不满，这些小插曲都会成为最珍贵的纪念品。

（二）节日给活动参与者带来快乐

洛阳牡丹节也给活动

①From http://blog.sina.com.cn/s/blog_4e4148ea01016j75.html.

①节选自：http://blog.sina.com.cn/s/blog_4e4148ea01016j75.html。

参与者带来了快乐，以下这位活动参与者的经历颇有代表性[1]。

瀍河回族区马沟村村民吕耐烦20多年来一直热爱文艺表演，在第27届、28届洛阳牡丹文化节期间，因参加牡丹舞表演，她与牡丹文化节结下了不解之缘。"大约从1986年开始，每年的牡丹文化节期间，我都会参加村里组织的扭秧歌、腰鼓表演。"吕耐烦说。

2009年第27届牡丹文化节，洛阳市首创的牡丹舞成为当届牡丹文化节的一大亮点，吕耐烦也有幸加入了那次千人表演牡丹舞的团队。她说，那是她第一次参加市里组织的牡丹文化节表演活动，现在回想起来还很激动。当时马沟村的表演队伍有40余人，其中有40多岁的中年人，也有和自己一样

[1]以下内容节选自：http://news.lyd.com.cn/system/2012/04/11/010074866.shtml。

participants, which is demostrated by the typical example below[1].

Lü Naifan is a resident of Magou Village, Chanhe District of Hui Minority and has been fond of dance for more than twenty years. She participated the peony dance show of the 27th and 28th peony cultural festivals and has a special feeling towards the peony festival. "I had participated the yangge dance and waist drum performance organized by our village every year during the festival since 1986." Lü said.

For the 27th peony festival in 2009, organizers created one-thousand-people peony dance, which was quite an eye-catcher. Lü was chosen as a member of the dance team. She said that it was her first time to participate in performances organized by Luoyang government and she still felt excited when she recalled it now. More than forty dancers were selected from her village. Some of them were around forty years old and others, like her, were in their sixties. Being able to participate in such an

[1] From http://news.lyd.com.cn/system/2012/04/11/010074866.shtml.

important activity of peony festival, they all worked very hard. They began to learn the dance steps every day in Magou Primary School in early March. "The steps were not that difficult to learn one by one, but we needed to cooperate and coordinate with others, so it was still hard for us." At that time, it was very cold and often windy. They had to run several hundred meters in the playground before learning. Though they usually started at 1 p.m, sometimes to make sure that all learners dance well, they would not leave even when it was dark. In April 2009, when the peony dance was first performed in Wangcheng Park, these dancers drew great attention. Lü said that she had never seen such a big show before. The dancers there were in nine different colors. Lü was wearing yellow clothes with

60多岁的老年人。不过，能参加牡丹文化节的重要表演活动，大家都排练得很卖力。从2009年3月初开始，吕耐烦和表演队的乡亲们一起，每天到当时的马沟村小学大院里排练。"牡丹舞的舞蹈动作并不算复杂，但讲求整体配合、协调，这对我们这些业余表演者来说，还是有点难度。"吕耐烦说。3月初的洛阳气温还比较低，时常刮起冷飕飕的风。为了让身体热乎些，大家都是在场地里跑几圈之后再开始排练。一般每天13时就开始排练，有时为了排练好一个动作，直到天黑了大家还不肯走。2009年4月初，首次公开亮相的牡丹舞表演在周王城广场拉开大幕，千名表演者在现场同台演出，格外引人注目。吕耐烦回忆说，那一年的表演盛况是自己过去从未见过的。现场的千名表演者穿着9种色系服装。自己所在方阵的表演者们穿着黄色上衣，手捧粉色"牡丹花"花束，表演展示了"牡

丹"由发芽、开花到怒放的情景，引得现场观众爆发出阵阵掌声。

2010年第28届牡丹文化节闭幕式上，吕耐烦再次参加了千人表演的牡丹舞。吕耐烦说，第二次参加表演，心里仍然很激动，牡丹文化节让我舞出了青春。

二、促进了传统文化的传承与传播

节日是地区文化集中展示的平台，而洛阳牡丹文化节随着30余年的发展，已成为洛阳地区甚至是中华文化传承与传播、展示与宣传的一个大舞台。每年的洛阳牡丹节，都会集中展示一批河洛地区非物质文化遗产，举办群众喜闻乐见的民间文化活动表演。社会各界也纷纷在花会期间举办花车巡游、牡丹婚典、全民体育月、牡丹书画展、邮票发行、牡丹灯会、万人交友会、诗歌朗诵会、体育舞蹈邀请赛等丰富多彩的文

an artificial pink peony flower bouquet in her hands. She and other team members showed how peony bud, grow and bloom, receiving sustained applause.

In the closing ceremony of 28th Peony Cultural Festival, Lü participated in the one-thousand-people peony dance again. Though this was her second time to perform, she still felt very excited. She said, "The peony festival makes me regain my youth."

2.Promote the inheritance and spread of traditional culture

Festival is an important way to show regional culture. After thirty years' development, Luoyang peony cultural festival has become a grand stage for Luoyang and even China to spread and promote its traditional culture. Every peony festival exhibits a series of Heluo intangible cultural heritage works and holds many popular folk performances. Organizations of different sectors also conduct various activities including float parade, peony wedding ceremony, sports month, peony calligraphy works and painting exhibition, issue of peony stamps, peony lantern show, blind date, poetry reading and sports dance invitation tournament. These activities draw many citizens and visitors to participate, greatly enhance Luoyang's image, and make peony cultural festival a new business card of Luoyang. The festival becomes peony's festival and people's festival, gradually forming a festival culture featured by "festival of people, festival of fashion, festival of recreation and festival of happiness". As the cultural elements of peony festival become more and more apparent, its unique culture brand has been established.

During July 11th to 12th, 2010, Liu Yuzhu, head of the Cultural Industries Department of the Ministry of Culture visited Luoyang to see the development of Luoyang peony festival and cultural industries. Liu Yuzhu said that Luoyang should make efforts to promote Luoyang peony festival as one of the cultural brands and cultural festivals with most international influence in five to ten years, so that it could be a channel to show the spirit of Chinese people, a bridge for the exchanges between China and the world, and a large cultural festival with continuing international influence. To achieve this goal, Luoyang needs to combine its rich historical and cultural resources with modern culture in future peony festivals to show the spirits of contemporary Chinese people, integrate every peony festival with

体活动，极大地满足了市民和游客的参与需求。接连不断的花会主题活动极大地提升了洛阳的城市形象，使牡丹文化节成为洛阳新的城市名片。花会也真正成为"牡丹的盛会、人民的节日"，逐渐形成了以"人文花会、时尚花会、休闲花会、狂欢花会"为主要内涵的花会文化，洛阳牡丹文化节的文化性日益凸显，独具特色的文化品牌已经形成。

2010年7月11日至12日，文化部文化产业司司长刘玉珠一行来洛阳，调研洛阳牡丹花会和文化产业发展状况。刘玉珠提出，要力争通过5年至10年努力，将洛阳牡丹花会提升为国内最具国际影响力的文化节会和文化品牌之一，使之成为展示当代中国人精神风貌的平台、中国与世界进行文化交流的平台，成为具有持续国际影响力的盛大文化节庆活动。为此，在今后的举办过程中，要把洛阳深厚的历史文化资源同当今文化迅猛发展结合起来，使之成为展示当代中国人精神风貌的平台；每一届花会都要同国家文化活动结合起来，成为国家文化活动的缩影；花会要与文化产业紧密结合，开拓更多、更好的文化活动，促进文化产业发展；要与扩大中国在世界上的影响力尤其是文化影响力结合起来，让花会成为中国与世界进行文化交流的平台；要通过花会活动，提升全民审美情趣和文化素质。①

2011年，在由中国人类学民族学研究会、国际节庆协会主办的"2011优秀民族节庆"推选活动中，中国洛阳牡丹文化节被评为"最具国际影响力节庆"。

national cultural activities to make the festival a epitome of Chinese cultural activities, combine the festival with cultural industries to create more and better cultural activities and promote the development of cultural industries, integrate the festival's influence with the influence of China in the world, especially China's cultural influence to make it a channel for cultural exchanges between China and the world, and promote people's aesthetic taste and cultural cultivation though the festival.①

Luoyang Peony Cultural Festival of China was awarded as Festival with the Most International Influence in 2011 China National Festival Summit, which was organized by International Festivals & Events Association and China Union of Anthropological and Ethnological Sciences.

---

①节选自：http://www.henan.gov.cn/zwgk/system/2010/07/13/010203269.shtml。

①Selected from: http://www.henan.gov.cn/zwgk/system/2010/07/13/010203269.shtml.

Protect and inherit Chinese culture

（一）文化的保护与传承

Chinese traditional culture is extensive and profound with a long history. As the ancient capital of thirteen dynasties, Luoyang boasts rich traditional culture. However, faced with the impact of modern civilization and technology, many scholars are afraid that traditional Chinese culture may degrade or disappear. Luoyang peony festival, by combining peony culture, regional culture and ethnic traditional

我国传统文化历史悠久、博大精深，洛阳作为十三朝古都，更是积累了厚重的传统文化内涵。但是在现代文明与高速发展的科技社会的冲击之下，不少学者都担心我国传统文化的退化与消失。然而，洛阳牡丹文化节的举办，

将牡丹文化、地区文化与民族传统文化融合在一起，尤其是在节日活动中所展现出来的传统元素与民族精神，使得传统文化的传承有了一个新的渠道。多姿多彩的节日活动不仅丰富了节日内容，烘托了节日气氛，更加集中展示了洛阳甚至是中国悠久灿烂的古国文明和博大精深的民俗文化。人们通过对节日的参与，领略蕴含于节日中的文化内涵，其实也是对我国传统文化的一种回归体验，可促进对自我民族文化的再认识。

2002年第20届洛阳牡丹花会上表演了一出"中国洛阳武皇十万宫廷乐舞"的节目。该曲目原本是武则天在洛阳请人精心打造的歌舞乐，后因历史变迁无人传承等原因而逐渐消亡。为活跃花会文化，拯救传统洛阳地方文化，洛阳市聘请音乐家和戏曲家对该曲谱进行整理，筛选出了《嵩山

culture together, and exhibiting traditional culture and national spirits through various activities, provides a new channel for the inheritance and spread of Chinese culture. Its diverse activities not only enrich the content of festival, make it more popular and exciting, but also show the great ancient civilization and rich folk culture of Luoyang and China. By participating in these activities, visitors and citizens have a taste of the connoted cultural meaning, gain a new experience for Chinese traditional culture, and know better of the national culture.

The 20th Luoyang Peony Festival in 2002 held Luoyang Imperial Dance of Empress Wu. Its songs and dances were originally made by Empress Wu when she was in Luoyang. But later due to the change of dynasties and lack of inheritance, they were gradually forgotten and no longer played. To enrich the culture of peony festival and protect traditional local culture, Luoyang government invited musicians and dramatists to recompose several songs based on original score. These experts arranged *Expressing Feeling on Mountain Song*, *Wu Visits Garden in Spring*, *The Charm of Tang*, *Ode to Peace*, etc.. When the songs were played in the festival, they received high praise from people of all sectors and were named "living fossil of music" by musicians.

Besides, during the peony festival, Wangcheng Park, one of the peony appreciating sites in Luoyang holds large ancient costume show called Welcoming Guests in Zhou Etiquette every year. Visitors there can enjoy a sight feast and experience the etiquette culture of the Zhou Dynasty while appreciating rare peony flowers. After three thunderous salvos, two teams of "soldiers" holding high colorful flags and wearing sword walk out from the front gate of Wangcheng Park and perform Bronze Sword Dance and Zhou Flag's Dance. Beside them are "peony fairies" wearing flowers on the head and

抒怀》《媚娘游春》《唐韵》《颂太平》等曲目作为经典，在牡丹花会上演绎，引起了社会各界的广泛好评，音乐界人士把其比喻为"音乐活化石"。

牡丹文化节期间，赏花景点之一的王城公园有一个保留节目——大型古装演艺活动"周礼迎宾"。游客们在观赏各种名贵牡丹花之余，还能享受一场精彩的视觉盛宴，感受古王朝的礼仪文化。随着三声震天炮响，两队高擎彩旗、腰佩宝剑的"武士"从王城公园正门鱼贯而出，跳起青铜剑舞

和大周旗舞，头戴鲜花的"牡丹仙子"则在一旁跳着王城迎宾舞。随后，礼乐齐鸣，锣鼓喧天，礼花绽放，"周武王"率"周公""召公"和"周成王"走出大门，观赏歌舞，并向游人频频致意。武王凯旋、王城定鼎、礼乐安邦和王城天香等一幕幕场景，再现了周王迎宾的宏大场面，浓缩了泱泱周王朝的王城文化。

（二）文化的传播与交流

洛阳牡丹节每年接待游客数以万计，许多其他省市地区甚至是国外的游客都专程赶来参与节日。游客们对于丰富多彩、精彩纷呈的节日活动都赞不绝口，对于其中所展现的文化内涵也表示欣赏与认同。而通过电视、网络等现代媒体传播技术，牡丹节也越来越走向大众、走向全国、走向世界。因此，洛阳牡丹节对于牡丹文化、洛阳文化以及中华民族传统文化的宣传、传播与交流作出了很大的贡献。

performing Guest Welcoming Dance. After that with loud salvos, deafening sound of drums and beautiful fireworks, Empire Wu of the Zhou Dynasty walks out with Duke Zhou, Duke Shao and Empire Cheng, all of whom are played by actors. They enjoy the songs and dances and send their greetings to visitors. The show's different parts, including the triumphant return of Empire Wu, tripod caldron built in Wangcheng, etiquettes to pacify state, peony of Wangcheng and so on, reproduce grand scenes when Empire Zhou welcomed guests and show the rich culture of the Zhou Dynasty.

Cultural exchanges and transmission

Every year hundreds of thousand visitors from China and abroad come to Luoyang and participate in festival activities. They speak highly of these diversified and interesting events and show their understanding and appreciation towards the cultural connotations. With the help of modern media such as TV and Internet, Luoyang peony festival becomes more and more popular and influential in China and the overseas. It has made a great contribution to the promotion, transmission and exchanges of peony culture, Luoyang culture and Chinese traditional culture.

Zhang Zhutang, vice president of China International Artist Association, vice president of China International Painting and Calligraphy Research Institute, and vice president of Cross-strait Cultural Exchange Association Union, was born in Xiangcheng, Henan Province. He was invited as the special guest in the opening ceremony of the first Luoyang Peony Festival in 1983. Though he was born in Henan, it was his first time to see peony. These red, yellow and black peony flowers were a big eye-opener for him and he was full of praises. As most of Zhang's life was spent in Xinjiang, where most places are Gobi or deserts with few flowers, suddenly seeing so many beautiful and gorgeous peony flowers, Zhang was quite surprised

张柱堂，中国国际书画研究院副院长、海峡两岸文化交流协会副会长，原籍河南项城，在1983年首届洛阳牡丹花会上担任开幕式特邀嘉宾。虽然祖籍是河南，但那一次却是他第一次看到牡丹。红牡丹、黄牡丹、黑牡丹，姹紫嫣红，让他大开眼界、赞不绝口。由于长期生活在新疆，那里多是戈壁、沙漠，野花都很少，突然看到这么多雍容华贵的牡丹，张柱堂难掩惊喜之情。

人多、场面火爆，是首届洛阳牡丹花会给他留下的印象。"我们新疆地广人稀，即使开大会，也看不到这么多人。"张柱堂笑着说。回新疆之后，张柱堂在《新疆信息报》头版突出位置刊发2000多字的通讯《洛阳牡丹甲天下》，称赞"洛阳是花的世界、花的海洋"。这篇文章在新疆读者中引发了"洛阳牡丹热"，不少读者给张柱堂写信，询问洛阳牡丹、花会时间等情况。第2届、第3届牡丹花会，很多新疆游客到洛阳看牡丹。2012年第30届洛阳牡丹文化节，张柱堂再次赴会。一下火车，洛阳新区宽广的街道、时尚的楼宇、修剪一新的花木、古色古香的园林，都让张柱堂兴奋不已。听说洛阳正在打造国际文化旅游名城，张柱堂非常赞同。他说，洛阳是千年帝都，历史文化积淀异常丰厚。宋代以前，洛阳作为中国政治、经济、文化中心，一直是中华文明的"文化名片"；丝绸之路直通西域和欧洲各国，河洛文化对以龟兹文化为代表的西域文化影响很深。

and delighted. Huge crowds of people and gorgeous flowers are the impressions he got from the first peony festival. "Xinjiang has vast land and a few population. Even in a big meeting, you can not see so many people." Zhang said with a smile. When back in Xinjiang, he published a two-thousand-word report "Luoyang's peony is the best in China" on the front page of *Xinjiang News*, praising Luoyang as the world of flowers and sea of flowers. This reports drew many readers' attention. They wrote to Zhang and asked for more information about Luoyang peony and the peony festival. Many of them even went to Luoyang to appreciate peony flowers during the second and third peony festivals. In 2012, Zhang went back to Luoyang again to attend the 30th Luoyang Peony Festival. The moment he got off the train, he was very surprised and excited by the broad street, fashionable buildings, tidy flowers and trees, and gardens with antique beauty in the new district of Luoyang. When he heard that Luoyang was trying to develop itself as a famous international tourist city with rich culture, he highly agreed. He said, "Luoyang is an ancient capital with more than one thousand years' history and has abundant historical and cultural resources. Being the political, economic and cultural center of China before the Song Dynasty, Luoyang was the cultural symbol of Chinese civilization. Besides, as Silk Road connected China, the Central Asia and the European countries, Luoyang and Heluo culture had a deep influence on the culture of west regions, which was represented by Qiuci culture in Xinjiang.

I think promoting Heluo culture in Xinjiang and studying the relationship between Heluo culture and Qiuci culture are very important to national unity and harmony. I would like to be an envoy between Heluo culture and Qiuci culture, making my own contribution of promoting Heluo culture in Xinjiang."

3.Push forward regional economic development and opening up

As a traditional folk festival in Luoyang, Luoyang peony festival is a platform for traditional culture

"我认为，在新疆宣传、弘扬河洛文化，研究河洛文化和龟兹文化的血脉渊源，对促进民族团结、民族和谐有着重要意义。我个人则希望能成为河洛文化和龟兹文化的使者，为在新疆弘扬河洛文化尽一点微薄之力！"张柱堂说。

三、带动了地区经济的发展与对外开放

洛阳牡丹花节是洛阳的传统民俗节日，是传统

文化的集中展示平台，也是洛阳对外开放的重要窗口。"花会搭台，经贸唱戏"，从1985年起，洛阳连续20多年借助花会平台举办经济技术交流暨贸易洽谈会等大型经贸活动，项目成交额达800多亿元，其中利用外资40多亿美元，不仅对发展经济起到了重要作用，而且大大增强了洛阳和河南在国内外的知名度。2008年第26届洛阳牡丹花会对外经济技术合作项目签约共签约合同项目88个，投资总额达449.7亿元，其中市外资金386.2亿元。签约项目中有外商投资项目13个，投资总额11.8亿美元，合同外资金额9.6亿美元。

（一）推动了洛阳城市基础设施建设的完善

随着洛阳牡丹花会的发展，洛阳市以及周边地区的基础设施建设也在不断地完善，尤其在交通设施建设、环境美化与绿化、旅游设施建设等方面。政府根据每年花会的

exhibition and also an important media of Luoyang's opening up to the outside world. "Using peony festival as the showcase for economy and trade" is the slogan of Luoyang government. Since 1985, Luoyang has conducted many economic and trade events like trade fairs and economic exchanges during more than twenty peony festivals. The total volume of trade reached more than eighty billion *yuan* and the utilization of foreign capital totaled more than four billion US dollars. This not only helps to promote economic development, but also increases Luoyang and Henan's influence domestically and globally. The 26th Luoyang Peony Festival in 2008 witnessed 88 economic and technical cooperation project contracts signed. Thirteen of them were invested by foreign enterprises, with investment totaling 1.18 billion US dollars and contract amount reaching 960 million US dollars. The total investment during the festival was 44.97 billion *yuan*, with 38.62 billion *yuan* from places out of Luoyang.

Improve Luoyang's infrastructure

With the development of Luoyang peony festivals, the infrastructure of Luoyang and its adjacent suburbs have been improved, especially in terms of environmental greening, transportation, and tourist facilities. Every year, based on the characteristics and need of peony festival, Luoyang government invests and constructs a series of tourist and municipal service facilities, peony festival projects, and transport facilities. Because of the festival, peony bridge, peony street, peony square, peony hotel, City of Peony Hotel and other peony related buildings come into being, highlighting the cultural connotation of peony, adding new scenic spots, offering fashionable elements for peony festivals, and making great changes to Luoyang.

Advance related industries' development

The success of Luoyang peony festival not only boosts regional economy, but also promotes related industries' development. Take peony industry for example. Under the propelling of peony festival, research on peony and peony planting has entered a new era. The research team of Luoyang peony quickly expands, publishing nearly one hundred scientific and technological achievements, and

特点及需要，都会投资建设一批旅游和市政设施项目，集中力量完成一批"花会工程"。牡丹桥、牡丹大道、牡丹广场、牡丹大酒店、牡丹城宾馆等一批以牡丹为标志的桥梁、文化广场、宾馆、饭店等建筑物，在牡丹文化节中应运而生，突出了牡丹文化的内涵，为城市增添了一个个新的景观，为牡丹文化节增添了时尚文化元素，使洛阳市的城市环境发生了巨大的变化。

（二）带动了相关产业的发展

洛阳牡丹节的成功举办，推动了地区经济的发展，并带动了相关产业的兴起与发展。如对洛阳牡丹产业的推动，使对牡丹的研究、繁育与栽培技术更上一个新的台阶。在牡丹文化节的带动下，洛阳牡丹科研队伍迅速壮大，近百项牡丹科技成果问世，已建立起国内规模最大、品种最多的牡丹基因库。针对牡丹花期较短，经过牡丹科技工作者多年的不懈努力，已具备了较成熟的牡丹花期控制技术和四季开花技术，使牡丹的盛花期由原来的11天延长至目前的40天。洛阳市把牡丹产业作为农业六大主导产业之一，推行标准化生产，建成牡丹标准化生产基地14个，产品销往全国各地和日本、法国等20多个国家和地区，年销牡丹100余万株。同时，还带动了以牡丹为元素的特色产品的开发、生产与销售，如牡丹瓷、牡丹枕、牡丹饼、牡丹茶、牡丹精油、牡丹护肤品等，年产值近亿元。另外，每年数以百万计的游客来洛阳参加牡丹节，也带动了洛阳地区旅游产业的发展，使旅游业成为洛阳市最具发展潜力的产业之一。

（三）促进了洛阳对外开放的程度

每届洛阳牡丹花节都遵循"以花为媒、广交朋友、宣传洛阳、发展洛阳"的宗旨，以花会为舞

establishing China's largest peony gene pool with most species. As the original flowering period of peony is very short, researchers have worked diligently for many years and managed to lengthen the flowering period from eleven days to current forty days by using mature florescence control and perpetual bloom techniques. Now peony industry is regarded by the government as one of the six leading agricultural industries in Luoyang. Peony standardized production has been introduced and fourteen production bases are established with more than one million tree peonies produced every year. They are sent to places all over China and more than 20 foreign countries and regions, including Japan and France. The development, production and sales of peony related products also grow quickly. The annual output value of peony china, peony pillow, peony pancake, peony tea, peony essential oil and peony skin care products totals nearly one hundred million yuan. Besides, with hundreds of thousand visitors coming to peony festival every year, tourism in Luoyang develops quickly and has become one of the most promising industries in Luoyang.

Enhance Luoyang's opening up to the outside world

Every Luoyang peony festival follows the principle of "Meet more friends while appreciating flowers; Promote and develop Luoyang." As a stage letting the world know better about Luoyang and making Luoyang merged into the world, it effectively enhances Luoyang's opening up to the outside world. During the peony festival, many large economic and trade events like trade fair, economic and technical cooperation projects, industrial fair and technological invention fair have been held in consecutive years, enabling products of Luoyang to be sold in overseas markets. Besides, as the image ambassador of Luoyang, peony has been planted in more than twenty countries, including Great Britain, U.S., France, Germany, Australia, Holland, Belgium and Singapore, enjoying a high reputation in the world. Because of peony, Luoyang has established friendships with Sukagawa of Japan, Tours in France, Plovdiv of Bulgaria, La Crosse in U.S., Buyeo County of Republic of Korea, and Tolyatti of Russia. Luoyang is also the sister city of

台，打开了"让世界了解洛阳，让洛阳走向世界"的大门，有力地推动了洛阳的对外开放。借助花会平台，洛阳市连续多年举办经济技术暨贸易洽谈会、工业品展销会、科技成果展会等大型经贸活动。通过花会搭台，洛阳市的出口产品远销到多个国家和地区。作为洛阳的形象使者，牡丹在英国、美国、法国、德国、澳大利亚、荷兰、比利时、新加坡等20多个国家生根开花，声名远

播。另外，通过以花为媒，洛阳市积极发展对外友好合作，先后与日本须贺川市、法国图尔市、保加利亚普罗夫迪夫市、美国拉克罗斯市、韩国扶余郡、俄罗斯的陶里亚蒂市缔结了友好关系；与北京西城区、上海杨浦、青岛、泉州等9个市（区）结为友好市（区）。牡丹花会使洛阳对外开放的形象更加优化、更加鲜活，真正成为洛阳走向世界的桥梁和让世界了解洛阳的名片。

Beijing Xicheng District, Shanghai Yangpu District, Qingdao, Quanzhou, and other five cities of China. Making Luoyang's image more lively and beautiful, peony festival becomes a real bridge for Luoyang to be merged into the world and a business card introducing Luoyang to the outside world.

第四章 中国其他地区的牡丹节

中国人爱牡丹，牡丹几乎遍植我国国土，而牡丹文化也深植在我国民族文化与民族精神之中。春日牡丹竞芳菲，每年春季，除牡丹花都洛阳外，我国其他的牡丹主要栽培地区都有牡丹花节，借此平台来展现牡丹之美，弘扬中华传统文化。

Chapter Four

Peony Festivals in Other Regions of China

Because of Chinese people's love for peony, peony is planted almost all over China. Its culture is also deeply rooted in Chinese culture and spirit. In spring, blooming peony flowers look beautiful and gorgeous. Besides the capital of peony, Luoyang, many other major peony planting regions also held peony festival, to present the beauty of peony, and promote Chinese culture.

1 菏泽国际牡丹节
Heze International Peony Festival

Heze, named Caozhou in ancient times, started to plant peony during the reign of Jiaqing of the Ming Dynasty. With more than four hundred years' peony planting history, it is one of the four major peony planting places in China[1]. Heze peony is featured by straight stem, luxuriant leaves, and elegant flowers, and is praised as the top grade of peony species. Pu Songling, a famous novelist of the Qing Dynasty, once mentioned that peony in Caozhou was the best in Shandong in his *Strange Tales from a Scholar's Studio*. In 2000, Heze was titled as County of Peony in China and in 2006 it was awarded as City of Peony in China. In 2012, after the application of Heze government and the inspection of experts from China Flower Association, Heze won the title The Capital of Peony in China according to The Naming

菏泽，古称曹州，其牡丹栽培始于明代嘉靖年间，至今已有400多年的历史，是我国牡丹四大产地[1]之一。菏泽牡丹的特点是枝干挺拔，叶繁茂多姿，花雍容华贵，被誉为观赏牡丹之上品。蒲松龄在其《聊斋志异》里有"曹州牡丹甲齐鲁"之说。2000年，菏泽被中国花卉协会命名为"中国牡丹之乡"。2006年，菏泽被评为"中国牡丹城"。2012年，根据《中国花卉协会命名授牌管理办法》，经菏泽市人民政府申报，

---

[1]The four major peony planting places in China are Luoyang, Henan province, Heze, Shandong province, Pengzhou, Sichuan province and Changshu, Jiangsu province.

[1]我国牡丹四大产地是：河南洛阳、山东菏泽、四川彭州和江苏常熟。

中国花卉协会组织专家考察、评审，决定命名菏泽市为"中国牡丹之都"。著名书法家舒同曾为菏泽牡丹挥毫题下"曹州牡丹甲天下"，溥杰先生也曾经为菏泽牡丹留下过"天下第一香"的墨宝。

菏泽是现在世界上种植面积最大、品种最多的牡丹生产基地、科研基地、出口基地和观赏基地。2012年，菏泽牡丹栽培面积已达12万亩，大型牡丹苗木繁育基地30多处，反季节牡丹温室催花大棚200多个，年产标准化牡丹观赏种苗1000余万株，牡丹四季催花200万盆，牡丹鲜切花400万枝。菏泽牡丹远销日本、美国、韩国、俄罗斯、法国、荷兰、澳大利亚等30多个国家和地区。菏泽牡丹由过去的单一观赏、药用逐步走上鲜切花、"不凋花"、深加工等全方位发展的综合开发生产之路，牡丹籽油、牡丹酒、牡丹茶、牡丹食用菌已开发成功，牡丹营养食品、牡丹日用品正在深层次研发中。

Regulations of China Flower Association. Shu Tong, a famous calligrapher in China once wrote "Caozhou peony is the best in China" and another well-known calligrapher, Fu Jie also wrote "The first fragrance of China" for Heze peony.

Heze now has the world's largest peony planting base, research base, export base and viewing base with the most peony species. Its peony planting area reaches about 120 thousand *mu* (8000 hectares), and the number of its large peony planting bases totals more than 30. There are also more than two hundred greenhouses for peony planting in winter. Every year, Heze produces more than ten million tree peonies, two million pots of blooming peony flowers in four seasons, and four million peony flowers. They are sold to more than thirty foreign countries and regions like Japan, America, Republic of Korea, Russia, France, Holland, and Australia. Heze peony industry has been developed from merely planting peony for ornamentation and drug use to a comprehensive utilization of peony. Fresh cutting flowers, dried flowers, peony seed oil, peony wine, peony tea and peony edible mushroom are being sold in market. Other products like peony food and peony daily use commodities are being developed.

Since 1992, Heze Peony Festival has been successfully held for twenty-one times. It began to be co-hosted by Shandong Provincial Tourism Administration and Heze government in 2004, the level of which is only inferior to Luoyang Peony Festival. The 2012 Heze International Peony Festival chose "Romantic Flower Capital, Dreamy City Heze" as its slogan, and "Heze peony flowers blooming in the world" as the theme. It had three major festival events: the opening ceremony, City of Peony festival gala, and China Peony Arrangement Works Exhibition; three economic activities: investment and trade fair, property fair, and food expo; ten tourist activities: Forum of the Cooperation of Shandong, Jiangsu, Henan, and Anhui, Heze Kanghui Travel Show, Rural Culture Arts Festival & Square Show, spring long-distance race, national flower wedding ceremony, outstanding local drama show, International Free Combat Competition & World King of Fight Competition, Predestined Love in the end of April Blind Date, Peony Appreciating in Caozhou, and Zhuizi Drama Appreciation; and nineteen other activities: Famous Calligraphy Works and Painting Exhibition, Han Yi Shen Fei (elegant calligraphy and flying spirit) Calligraphy Works Show from Zigong, Sichuan and Heze, Shandong, Grotesque Stones, Root Carvings and Bonsai Works Exhibition from

自1992年起，菏泽国际牡丹花节已成功举办了21届。2004年起，由山东省旅游局和菏泽市人民政府共同主办此节庆活动，节日规格仅次于中国洛阳牡丹文化节。2012年菏泽国际牡丹花节以"烂漫花都，梦幻菏泽"为宣传口号，以"菏泽牡丹向世界绽放"为主题，安排了主题节庆活动3项：大型文艺演出（开幕式）、"相约牡丹城"专场庆典晚会、中国牡丹插花艺术展，经贸活动3项：投资贸易洽谈会、住房与房地产博览会、美食博览会，文体旅游活动10项："鲁苏豫皖区域协作"菏泽论坛暨"菏泽康辉旅游风情展"、农村文化艺术节暨大型广场文化展演、春季长跑赛、国花婚礼大典、地方戏曲精品展演、国际散打赛暨世界搏击王者争霸赛、月末情缘相亲大会、曹州赏牡丹、听名家坠子等。除此以外，还安排了综合类与县区活动

19项：中国书画名家作品邀请展、"翰逸神飞"四川自贡·山东菏泽书法交流展、鲁苏豫皖奇石根雕盆景邀请展、牡丹花王大赛、传统武术项目大展演、斗鸡斗羊大赛、太极拳锦标赛、定陶仿山古庙会、"镜头中的精彩"大型摄影展等节日活动。

Shandong, Jiangsu, Henan, and Anhui, King of Peony Flowers Competition, Traditional Chinese Martial Arts Show, Cockfighting and Ram-fighting Show, Tai-Chi competition, Dingtao Fangshan Traditional Folk Fair, and Wonderful World in Camera: Photo Exhibition.

2 成都（彭州）牡丹花生态旅游节
Chengdu (Pengzhou) Peony Ecotourism Festival

Pengzhou, also named Tianpeng, is one of the major peony planting areas in China and was traditionally called the city of flowers. Originally growing in Danjing Mountain, Pengzhou peony began to be cultivated in the Tang Dynasty, and was as famous as Luoyang peony during the Song Dynasty. During the South Song Dynasty, Pengzhou peonies were very luxuriant and had the same fame as Luoyang peonies. Their stems were tall and straight with flowers lowering their head, beautifying the valley. Because of this, Pengzhou replaced Luoyang to be the peony planting center at that time. Lu You, a famous Song poet wrote in *Tianpeng Peony* that "In the central region, Luoyang peony is the best, while in Sichuan, Pengzhou peony is the best." In history, Pengzhou was the peony planting center of the southwest of China. Peony species there are very suitable for gardening and their flowers are highly multi-layered. Some even have more than 880 petals. Peony stems are tall and

彭州又名天彭，素有"花州"之称，为中国牡丹的主要原产地之一。彭州牡丹发源于丹景山，人工栽植观赏始于唐，至南宋时期，花特盛，以"天骄寻丈，倒叶垂华，绚烂山谷"的独特风格与洛阳牡丹齐名。彭州也一度取代洛阳，成为中国牡丹的栽培中心。陆游《天彭牡丹谱》云："牡丹在中州，洛阳为第一；在蜀，天彭为第一。"历史上，彭州是西南地区牡丹品种群的栽培中心，西南牡丹种群园艺化及花型演化程度相当高，花朵高度重瓣，多达880余瓣，植株高大，根型浅，耐湿热，深受历代名人赞誉。改革开放以来，牡丹花被定为彭州市市花。彭州以丹景山为发展传统名花的基地，建设了以牡丹观赏为特色的风景区丹景山，也被称为"中国西部花山"，每年4月上旬至5月下旬，山上山下的各色牡丹次第开放，非常让人惊艳。

1985年，彭州市将牡丹定为市花，并举办了首届彭州牡丹花会。至2012年，已连续举办了28届。现在，彭州牡丹花会已成为全国最大、最有影响的三大牡丹花会①之一。每年春天，彭州尤其是丹景山牡丹遍山漫野，千姿百态，游人如潮，纷至沓来。国际树木协会副主席G.L.奥斯蒂博士上山考察天彭牡丹，欣然题词赞誉这里为"人间天堂"。2012年第28届成都（彭州）牡丹花生态旅游节期间，丹景山开辟了蜀秀园、丹霞园、天香园、牡丹坪、大千园和金华园等12大牡丹观赏园区，并从

---

① 我国三大牡丹花会是洛阳牡丹花会、菏泽国际牡丹花会、彭州牡丹花会。

straight, and the roots are short, able to bear moist and warm climate. Therefore, it has been praised by many celebrities. Since the reform and opening up, peony was designated as the city flower of Pengzhou and Danjing Mountain was appointed as the base for traditional flowers planting. Having many unique peony appreciating zones, Danjing Mountain is called The Flower Mountain in the west of China. Every year, from early April to late May, different colored peony flowers blossom in succession, amazing all visitors there.

The First Pengzhou Peony Festival was held in 1985, when peony was designated as the city flower. Till now (2012), 28 peony festivals have been held and it gradually becomes one of the three largest and most influential peony festivals in China[1]. During the festival, peony flowers bloom all over Pengzhou, especially in Danjing Mountain with various colors and shapes, attracting countless visitors from home and abroad. After Doc. G. L. Osti, associate director of International Society of Agriculture, visited Tianpeng peony, he wrote that Pengzhou was "heaven on earth". During the 28th Chengdu (Pengzhou) Peony Tourism Festival in 2012, Danjing Mountain built 12 peony appreciating areas including Shuxiu (beauty of Sichuan) Garden, Danxia (red clouds) Garden, Tianxiang (celestial

---

[1] The three largest peony festivals in China are Luoyang Peony Festival, Heze International Peony Festival and Pengzhou Peony Festival.

fragrance) Garden, Mudan Ping (peony flowerbed), Daqian (boundless world) Garden and Jinhua (gold's glory) Garden, introducing nearly one hundred new peony species from Luoyang, Changshu, and Heze. Visitors there can appreciate about three million tree peonies of more than three hundred species including Danjing Hong (Danjing red), Da Ye Hong (big-leaf red), Wu Zhou Hong (five-continent red), Bai He Wo Xue (white crane on snow), and Pengzhou Zi (Pengzhou purple). The festival also held eight theme activities: peony exhibition, peony calligraphy works, photos and paintings exhibition, praying for blessing, tour in Jianjiang, food carnival, white cherry picking, bamboo shoots plucking, cold-water fish tasting, and Pengzhou tea drinking.

河南洛阳、江苏常熟和山东菏泽等地新引进牡丹品种近100个，在景区可观赏到丹景红、大叶红、五州红、白鹤卧雪和彭州紫等在内的300多个品种，总数达300万株的牡丹花开盛景。花会期间还开展了牡丹联展、牡丹书画摄影、祈福、涧江休闲主题游、美食狂欢节、采摘白樱桃、采摘春笋、品冷水鱼和品彭人古茶等八大主题活动。

3 中国（常熟）尚湖牡丹花会
Shanghu (Changshu) Peony Festival

常熟是我国江南地区第一个举办牡丹花会的城市，从1990年开始，常熟已经成功举办了22届牡丹花会。经过不断发展，常熟如今已形成了江南最为完备，也是规模最大的牡丹园，汇聚了洛阳、菏泽、彭州及常熟四地的九大色系、超过300个品种、5万多株的精品牡丹，开辟了中华牡丹园、德国、法国、瑞士、美国、日本等8个精品牡丹主题欣赏园。据统计，历届牡丹花会都吸引了数以万计的旅游爱好者前来参观，2012年第21届尚湖牡丹花会以"花俏江南，美丽假日"为主题，不

Changshu is the first city in regions south of the Yangtze River to hold peony festival. And it has held 22 peony festivals since 1990. After years' development, Changshu is now the largest peony garden with most peony species in regions south of the Yangtze River. It boasts more than fifty thousand precious tree peonies of more than three hundred species, whose nine major colors of peonies originated from Luoyang, Heze, Pengzhou and Changshu, and eight peony theme parks named as Peony of China, Germany, France, Switzerland, United States, Japan, etc. According to statistics, every Changshu Peony Festival attracted dozens of thousand visitors. The 21st Shanghu Peony Festival in 2012, themed as "Beautiful South China and Happy Holiday", not only had the refinement and beauty of former festivals, but also provided various activities and splendid sight experiences for visitors. Even those who went to the festival every year could

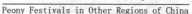
notice its novelty and creativity. During the festival, Yushan Shanghu Holiday Resort organized a series of activities like self-drive to appreciate flowers and the moon in the Yangtze River Delta, and peony boat parade. Visitors by participating in the festival activities and admiring beautiful scenery, enjoyed a great time there. Major activities held during the 21st Shanghu Peony Festival included Spring Tide: Drive to Appreciate Peony and the Moon, National Beauty and Celestial Fragrance: Miss Tourism Planet (East China) Qualification Tournament, Celestial Fragrance: Peony Fairy Parade, Glamorous Time: Peony of China and Abroad Exhibition, Magnificent South China and Yushan Shanghu: Scenery Picture Show, Floral South China: Peony Boat Parade, Vibing to the Music: Meeting of Music Lovers from Peony Allied Cities, Refined Taste of Seclusion: Life in Fushui Villa, Love in Shanghu: Blind Date and Elegant Orchid and Beautiful Music: *Peony Pavilion Show*.

仅延续了以往牡丹花会的精巧，还提供了更加丰富多彩的活动内容及不同凡响的视觉体验，让参观者有"年年看牡丹，岁岁大不同"的感受。同时，花会期间，虞山尚湖旅游度假区还举办了长三角自驾赏花月、牡丹花船巡游等一系列的活动，通过这些参与性较强的节庆活动以及更为浓郁的江南园景特色，给予游客全方位的美丽体验。第21届尚湖牡丹花会的主要活动有："春潮涌动"长三角自驾赏花月、"国色天香"环球旅游美皇后（华东）选拔赛、"天香竞艳"牡丹仙子巡游、"魅力年华"中外牡丹花道展示、"锦绣江南·虞山尚湖"四季风光图片展、"花俏江南"牡丹花船巡游、"声声抒怀"中国牡丹行联盟城市琴友雅集、"归隐雅趣"拂水山庄穿越体验、"情缘尚湖"大型相亲会、"幽兰雅韵"牡丹亭昆曲展演等。

除上述牡丹花节外，我国还有很多地区举办牡丹花节，如重庆市垫江县举办的中国·重庆垫江牡丹文化节、安徽省南陵县举办的中国（南陵）江南牡丹文化节、河北省柏乡县举办的中国汉牡丹文化节、山西省古县举办的中国·古县牡丹文化旅游节。

Besides above-mentioned peony festivals, there are also many places in China holding peony festivals, such as Dianjiang County in Chongqing, Nanling County of Anhui Province, Boxiang of Hebei Province, and Gu County of Shanxi Province.

The Postscript of *Chinese Festival Culture Series*

China has developed its splendid and profound culture during its long history of 5000 years. It has a vast territory, numerous ethnic groups as well as the colorful festivals. The rich festival activities have become the invaluable tourism resources. The traditional festivals, such as the Spring Festival, the Tomb-Sweeping Day, the Dragon Boat Festival, the Mid-Autumn Day and the Double-Ninth Festival as well as the festivals of ethnic minorities, are representing the excellent traditional culture of China and have become an important carrier bearing the spirits and emotions of the Chinese people, the spirit bond of the national reunification, national unity, cultural identity and social harmony, and an inexhaustible driving force for the development of the Chinese Nation.

In order to spread the excellent traditional culture of China and build the folk festival brand for our country, the Folk Festival Commission of the China Union of Anthropological and Ethnological Science (CUAES) has worked with the Anhui People's Publishing House to publish the *Chinese*

《中国节庆文化》丛书后记

上下五千年的悠久历史孕育了灿烂辉煌的中华文化。中国地域辽阔，民族众多，节庆活动丰富多彩，而如此众多的节庆活动就是一座座珍贵丰富的旅游资源宝藏。在中华民族漫长的历史中所形成的春节、清明、端午、中秋、重阳等众多传统节日和少数民族节日，是中华民族优秀传统文化的历史积淀，是中华民族精神和情感传承的重要载体，是维系祖国统一、民族团结、文化认同、社会和谐的精神纽带，是中华民族生生不息的不竭动力。

为了传播中华民族优秀传统文化，打造中国的优秀民族节庆品牌，中国人类学民族学研究会民族节庆专业委员会与安徽人民出版社合作，在国务院新闻办公室的大力支持下，决定联合出版大型系列丛书——《中国节庆文化》丛书。为此，民族节庆专委会专门成立了《中国节庆文化》丛书编纂委员会，邀请了国际节庆协会（IFEA）主席兼首席执行官史蒂文·施迈德先生、中国文联执行副主席冯骥才先生、中国人类学民族学研究会常务副会长周明甫先生、国家民委政研室副主任兼中国人类学民族学研究会秘书长黄忠彩先生、国家民委文宣司司长武翠英女士等担任顾问，由文化部民族民间文艺发展中心主任李松担任主编，十六位知名学者组成编委会，负责丛书的组织策划、选题确定、体例拟定和作者的甄选。随后，组委会在全国范围内，遴选了五十位节庆领域知名专家学者以及有着丰富实操经验的节庆策划师共同编著。

策划《中国节庆文化》丛书，旨在弘扬中国传统文化，挖掘本土文化和独特文化，展示中华民

Festival Culture Series under the support from the State Council Information Office. For this purpose, the Folk Festival Commission has established the editorial board of the *Chinese Festival Culture Series*, by inviting Mr. Steven Wood Schmader, the president and CEO of the International Festival and Events Association (IFEA); Mr. Feng Jicai, the executive vice-president of China Federation of Literary and Art Circles; Mr. Zhou Mingfu, the vice-chairman of the China Union of Anthropological and Ethnological Science (CUAES); Mr. Huang Zhongcai, the deputy director of the politics research office of the National Ethnic Affairs Commission, and the secretary-general of the China Union of Anthropological and Ethnological Science (CUAES); Ms. Wu Cuiying , the director of the Cultural Promotion Department of the National Ethnic Affairs Commission as consultants; Li Song, the director of the Folk Literature and Art Development Center of the Ministry of Culture as the chief editor; and 16 famous scholars as the members to organize, plan, select and determine the topics and determine the authors. After the establishment of the board, 50 famous experts and scholars in the field of festivals and the festival planners with extensive experiences have been invited to jointly edit the series.

The planning of the *Chinese Festival Culture Series* is to promote the traditional Chinese culture, explore the local and unique cultures, showcase the charms of the festivals of the Chinese Nation, express the gorgeous and colorful folk customs and create a festival image for cities. The target consumers of the series are the readers both at home and abroad who are interested in the festivals of China, and the purpose of the series is to promote the traditional culture and modern culture of China to the world and make the world know China in a better way by using the festivals as medium. The editorial board requests the editors shall integrate the theories into practice and balance the expertise and the popularity.

At present, the first part of the series will be published, namely the *Festivals in Spring*, and the editorial work of this part has been started in April, 2012 and completed in June, 2013. During this period of time, the editorial board has held six meetings to discuss with the authors and translators in terms of the compiling styles, outlines, first draft and translation to improve the draft and translation; and to consult with the publishing house in terms of the graphic design, editorial style and publishing schedule to improve the cultural quality of the series.

The first part *Festivals in Spring* is composed of 10 volumes to introduce 10 folk festivals of China from the first month to the third month of the Chinese Calendar, including the Spring Festival, the Lantern Festival, the Festival of February of the Second, the Festival of March the Third, the Tomb-Sweeping Day, the Peony Festival, the

族的节庆魅力，展现绚丽多姿的民俗风情，打造节庆城市形象。本丛书以对中国节庆文化感兴趣的中外读者为对象，以节庆活动为载体，向世界推广中国的传统文化和现代文化，让中国走向世界，让世界更了解中国。编委会要求每位参与编写者，力争做到理论性与实践性兼备，集专业性与通俗性于一体。

目前推出的是第一辑《春之节》，其编纂工作自2012年4月启动，2013年6月完成。期间编委会先后六次召开了专题会议，就丛书编纂体例、书目大纲、初稿、译稿与作者及译者进行研讨，共同修改完善书稿和译稿；就丛书的装帧设计、编辑风格、出版发行计划与出版社进行协商，集思广益，提高丛书的文化品位。

《春之节》共十册，分别介绍了中华大地上农历一月至三月有代表性的十个民族节庆，包括春节、元宵节、二月二、三月三、清明节、牡丹节、藏历年、壮族蚂蚜节、苗族姊妹节、彝族赛装节等，对每个节日的起源与发展、空间流布、节日习俗、海外传播、现代主要活动形式等分别进行了详细的介绍和深度的挖掘，呈现给读者的将是一幅绚丽多彩的中华节庆文化画卷。

这套丛书的出版，是民族节庆专业委员会和安徽人民出版社合作的结晶。安徽人民出版社是安徽省最早的出版社，有六十余年的建社历史，在对外传播方面走在全国出版社的前列；民族节庆专业委员会是我国节庆研究领域唯一的国家级社团，拥有丰富的专家资源和地方节庆资源。这套丛书的出版，实现了双方优势资源的整合。丛书的面世，若能对推动中国文化的对外传播，促进传统民族文化的传承与保护，展示中华民族的文化魅力，塑造节庆的品牌与形象有所裨益，我们将甚感欣慰。

掩卷沉思，《中国节庆文化》丛书凝聚着诸位作者的智慧和学养，倾注

Tibetan Calendar New Year, the Maguai Festival of the Zhuang People, the Sister Rice Festival, and the Saizhuang Festival of the Yi Ethnic Group. Each festival is introduced in detail to analyse its origin, development, distribution, customs, overseas dissemination and major activities, showing the readers a colorful picture about the Chinese festivals.

This series are the product of the cooperation between the Folk Festival Commission and the Anhui People's Publishing House. Anhui People's Publishing House is the first publishing house of its kind in Anhui Province, which has a history of more than 60 years, and has been in the leading position in terms of foreign publication. The Folk Festival Commission is the only organization at the national level in the field of the research of the Chinese festivals, which has rich expert resources and local festival resources. The series have integrated the advantageous resources of both parties. We will be delighted and gratified to see that the series could promote the foreign dissemination of the Chinese culture, promote the inheritance and preservation of the traditional and folk cultures, express the cultural charms of China and build the festival brand and image of China.

In deep meditation, the *Chinese Festival Culture Series* bears the wisdoms and knowledge of all of its authors and the great effort of the editors, and explains the splendid cultures of the Chinese Nation. We hereby sincerely express our gratitude to the members of the board, the authors, the translators, and the personnel in the publishing house for their great effort and to all friends from all walks of the society for their support. We hope you can provide your invaluable opinions for us to further promote the following work so as to show the world our excellent festival culture.

着编纂者的心血和付出，也诠释着中华民族文化的灿烂与辉煌。在此，真诚感谢各位编委会成员、丛书作者、译者、出版社工作人员付出的辛勤劳动，以及各界朋友对丛书编纂工作的鼎力支持！希望各位读者对丛书多提宝贵意见，以便我们进一步完善后续作品，将更加璀璨的节庆文化呈现在世界面前。

Editorial Board of
Chinese Festival Culture Series
December, 2013

《中国节庆文化》
丛书编委会
2013年12月